The Computer Dictionary

To Christine, Bill and William

The Computer Dictionary

Jon Wedge

Adam & Charles Black
London

ISBN 0-7136-2681-X

Published by A & C Black (Publishers) Limited
35 Bedford Row, London, WC1R 4JH

First published 1984

Wedge, Jon
The Computer dictionary
1. Computers–Dictionaries
2. Electronic data processing–Dictionaries
I. Title
001.64'03'21 QA76.15

Cover design: Gerald Rogers
Illustrations: Jim Barker (mostly from originals by Christine Wedge)
Phototypeset in 10/12pt Italia by Armitage Typo/Graphics Ltd, Huddersfield
Printed and bound in Great Britain at the Pitman Press, Bath

INTRODUCTION

There was once a Computer Person who found himself struggling to maintain his grip on the English language.

This Computer Person decided to see if he could explain the words that he used all day in such a way that a Reasonable Person could understand them.

He wanted to make computer terminology understandable to someone who did not wish to embark on a full computer education exercise.

He did not like working, so he also tried to ensure that reading his book would not seem like work to others.

When he had finished he had a long think about how successful the methodology had been, functionality-wise. Then he devoted some resource to having a beer or two.

He never did reach a conclusion, but here is the book.

CONTENTS

The main section contains general explanations and information. This is for reference, or for browsing through during dinner parties.

Words which are specifically explained in the dictionary are printed in **semibold type** the first time that they occur in a definition. This is not done for the very common words. **Semibold** is okay, but you can have too much of a good thing.

The Supplements are recorded separately because they are not the sort of thing which one would want to read accidentally.

They provide more detailed explanations for two of the more technical entries in the main section.

They are located at the back of the book.

Abort

To **abort** a program is to leave it all of a sudden. It is rather like leaving an office block by jumping out of the window.

You would only jump out of the office window if something was seriously wrong, like the building being on fire. Similarly the computer would only abort a program if something drastic had occurred, for example if the program had tried to multiply somebody's date of birth by their surname.

This should never happen of course, but neither should office blocks catch fire.

A variation on an abort is known as an 'Abend', for Aborted, Abnormal or Abandoned End. This is slightly more dignified, in that the program is able to do a bit of tidying up, say closing the **files,** before aborting.

This is broadly equivalent to clearing up your desk before jumping out of the window.

Absolute Addressing

When a program is being run the program instructions and the areas used for data occupy the memory of the computer.

Some types of instruction 'branch' the program to other instructions, while other types access the data areas. Both groups therefore need some means of 'addressing' the appropriate memory locations.

The most common addressing method allows the programmer to use **symbolic** names for the 'addressed' instructions and data areas. The **assembler, compiler** or **interpreter** works out the actual physical byte numbers within memory (see **symbolic addressing**).

Some languages also have **absolute addressing,** whereby the programmer works out and specifies the physical byte number of the 'addressed' data area or instruction for himself.

Doing this is really stupid. If additional instructions are later inserted in the program the original instructions and data areas may be displaced, thus ending up in different memory locations the next time that the program is used. The associated absolute addresses that the programmer originally specified are now wrong, and the program will not work correctly until they have all been changed.

There are only two justifications for absolute addressing. One is for those who are programming just for excitement and find that being permanently on the brink of disaster helps. The second applies to those who are seeking to prove that they cannot program in order to get promoted to **systems analyst.**

Acoustic Coupler

An **acoustic coupler** provides a slow but cheap means of transferring data between computers and 'intelligent' devices in a remote location. It does this by using ordinary telephone handsets.

The device could be a keyboard and printer, or a calculator-like box which has had information keyed into it specifically for transfer to the main computer.

The acoustic coupler consists of a box of electronic tricks – a kind of **modem** – with a couple of wobbly rubber coffee cups sitting on the top.

The wobbly rubber coffee cups are designed to hold the mouth- and ear-

pieces of a telephone handset. The acoustic coupler is also plugged into the computer or other device.

You have an acoustic coupler at each end of an ordinary telephone line. The data then goes between the device and the computer via the line, having been converted into an acoustic signal for the telephone-to-telephone part of its journey.

Of course acoustic signals and wobbly rubber coffee cups form a fair old obstacle course for even the fittest piece of data, which is why transfer speeds are relatively slow.

ADA

ADA is a high-level programming **language.** It was created to reduce the enormous amount of time spent on the development and maintenance of programs used by Western government defence departments.

Speculating on what the acronym ADA stands for is interesting, and in the right company can be worth a few quid in wagers.

There is plenty of scope because it is not an acronym at all. ADA was in fact named after the only child of Lord and Lady Byron, Ada Lovelace. In the 1840s Lady Lovelace consolidated and refined Babbage's work on computing engines and their use. She is sometimes called the first programmer.

ALGOL

ALGOL is a high-level **language** for use in scientific applications. The major design objective was to ensure that the language would be usable on a wide range of different computers.

ALGOL stands for ALGOrithmic Language, which is enough to put anyone off. This it has largely succeeded in doing.

Algorithm

An **algorithm** is the calculation required to resolve a complicated formula. In a computer an algorithm is worked out by a program.

Opinion varies as to how complicated a formula has to be to need an algorithm rather than a mere calculation to resolve it. Some would argue that nothing short of a program to work out which direction you should follow to arrive at Uranus in two years' time deserves the accolade of an algorithm. Others would use an algorithm to work out their winnings from £2 on the nose at 6-4 on.

Analyst/Programmer

An **analyst/programmer** performs the functions of both the **systems analyst** and the programmer. The two jobs involve specifying what a set of **application programs** should do, and actually writing the programs.

The problem is that the two jobs attract entirely different types of people. The analyst normally likes to deal with the outside world and would prefer not to get involved in the detail of what goes on inside the computer. The programmer, on the other hand, likes playing around on the computer and has a strong preference for being left well alone by the outside world.

An analyst/programmer is therefore usually either an analyst who has been forced to program or a programmer who has been forced to analyse.

It is easy to tell which is which.

The analyst prefers writing **specifications,** does it first, and then gradually simplifies it because trying to get the program to do all the things he originally specified is driving him crazy.

The programmer writes the program first because the only way he can get the specification correct is to finish the programming first.

Neither approach is ideal.

The other difficulty facing the analyst/programmer is that analysts habitually blame programmers if something goes wrong, and programmers habitually blame analysts. Things still go wrong for analyst/programmers. This is why so many of them drink too much.

Application Program

The **application program** is important in a computer system in the same way that speakers of some kind are important in a stereo system. Without it the computer is no use to anyone.

It is the application program that dictates what appears on the screen, what is printed, what is recorded on disk or cassette, what keyboard entries are required, what they need to be checked against, what they must be added to and so on and so on and so on and on, and it even decides when to stop and let another program have a go.

A Star Wars game on a home computer could be considered an application program, as could a payroll program running on a microcomputer, or a data-entry program running 40 screens with 40 operators on a **mainframe** system.

An application program can be written in any language. However, it will probably rely on **systems programs** to do the dirty work. For example, the application program might issue an instruction to write someone's payroll record to the payroll file on disk. It is the systems program's job to work out exactly where on the disk it should actually be written to.

The working out is quite important. It is no good burying a bone if you cannot find it again.

The application program, then, is what you see and use for a particular job. This makes it the computer's contact point with the outside world.

Array

See **DIM**.

ASCII

ASCII stands for the American Standard Code for Information Interchange. It is pronounced 'Askey' in tribute to that great English comedian, Arthur.

ASCII is one of two dominant coding systems (the other is **EBCDIC)** defining the combination of bits which represents each character. It is like a souped-up Morse code, using the on/off condition of bits instead of dots and dashes.

Each character normally has a byte devoted to it, though ASCII in fact only uses seven of the eight bits in a byte. (If you are not entirely sure what bits and bytes are, then be practical. Look them up now. This is going to get worse before it gets better.) The eighth bit is set to 'O'.

Seven bits provide 128 unique combinations, which allows for unique definitions of each letter, both lower and upper case, plus numbers, punctuation marks and symbols. This leaves a few for the computer's internal use (see **control characters).**

To illustrate the use of ASCII here's an example of what would be sent to the printer if the word 'Poppy' is to be printed. The **hexadecimal** notation is also given for completeness. You can ignore it for now if you like. However, if you do not know what hexadecimal is and you are not even curious, what on earth do you think you are doing reading up on ASCII?

CHARACTER	P	o	p	p	y
BITS SENT	01010000	01101111	01110000	01110000	01111001
HEXADECIMAL	50	6F	70	70	59

Incidentally, some weirdos know the entire ASCII code set by heart. I know I do. I like to brag about it, but it never seems to do me any good.

Assembler

See **assembly languages.**

Assembly Languages

Back in the good old days when men were men and programmers were programmers the programs were written and executed in the form of a glorified string of bits called **machine code.**

This made life easy for the computer and very difficult for the programmer.

As computers became more powerful, **assemblers, compilers** and **interpreters** were developed. These converted programs written in a language (see **source code**) into a form which could be run by the computer (see **object code**).

This made life a lot easier for the programmers, who could now write programs using symbols and real words rather than bit strings.

The many **assembly languages** (also referred to as 'assemblers') convert direct into machine code through the good offices of an assembler **utility program.** This proximity to the machine code makes them 'low-level' languages. If you need convincing, look at this sequence of Intel 8080 instructions, which come with equally incomprehensible comments:

```
MOV A,B      *Move register B to register A
ORA A        *Logical 'OR' on A using Accumulator contents
JNZ AGAIN    *If no bits are at zero jump to 'AGAIN'
```

See **languages** for a comparison of this kind of thing with boring high-level languages. The important thing here is that this is definitely one step up from a string of bits. It also allows use of **symbolic addressing,** which is a great step forward from raw machine code.

Nowadays virtually all machine code is first written in an assembly language. They certainly have a little more zap than your average high-level language.

'PRINT RESULT'. Call that programming?

Asynchronous Communication

Asynchronous communication is a method of sending data from one device to another.

The devices could be two computers, two telex machines, or a computer and a **peripheral.**

Asynchronous communication means that characters are sent individually, as and when they are ready. The devices at either end do not need to 'synchronise' on a consolidated block of characters such as is sent when using **synchronous communication.**

Characters sent asynchronously are like drips from a tap. Each drip has its own start and stop bits and because of this overhead it is not possible to achieve the data transfer speeds attainable with synchronous blocks. However, transfer speed is not exactly vital when the receiving device cannot handle data quickly, as is the case with most printers or telex machines.

ATM

An **ATM** is an Automatic Teller Machine. It is a machine which provides some of the services usually provided by a bank teller, or cashier.

The ATM lets you identify your account by the insertion of a plastic card. You verify that you are the authorised card user by entry of a number. This is called the PIN, or personal identification number.

The ATM is then able to look up your account record on the computer, check that the PIN is correct and, unfortunately, check how much money you have in the account.

Backing Storage

See **storage**.

Bar Codes

Bar codes are the curious black and white stripes that you see on cans of baked beans, or library tickets. You can also see one on the back of this book. If it is not there, somebody has changed the cover.

A bar code is simply another way of representing numbers and characters, each of which has a unique combination of stripes, defined by a coding system.

There are several different systems in common use; in most of these the stripes come in four varieties, thick and thin black, and thick and thin white.

Bar codes are used because they are easy to read into a computer using a special 'pen', or 'wand'. The pen works out for itself how fast it is being moved over the code from the first few stripes, which are the same in every code for which the pen is used. It can then convert the time it spends looking at black or white into the stripe pattern, and thus into the characters being represented.

It makes sure that the read was accurate using a **redundancy check** calculation. Most pens emit a beep to tell the operator that the read has worked.

Shortly after a friend of mine accidentally became a **technical programmer** with a **software house** he got involved in trying to get a prototype bar code reader to send the characters it had read into a Point of Sale **(POS)** computer. His role was to sit with someone else and say 'I see' or 'Oh dear' every once in a while.

He said that it was quite relaxing, because each time they blew up a prototype they had to wait ages for another one to arrive. This is all part of being at the forefront of technology.

Barrel Printers

See **printers.**

BASIC

BASIC is a simple high-level programming **language.** It is the most commonly used language for home and personal microcomputers, because it is easy to learn.

BASIC stands for Beginner's All-purpose Symbolic Instruction Code and was originally developed in Dartmouth College, New Hampshire, in 1965. It has since bred uncontrollably, and now there are literally hundreds of slightly different BASICs, having slightly different instruction sets.

You cannot have it both ways of course. BASIC may be easy to learn, but it is quite inadequate for getting many jobs done. Similarly, it is relatively easy to learn to fly a hang-glider, but a hang-glider is not much good for a real flying job like transporting 300 people from London to New York.

However, programming, even in BASIC, comes more naturally to some people than others . . .

I'm a middle-aged commuter
Who has bought a home computer
And has seen his lifestyle turned upon its head;
For since starting on this caper,
I've not seen a daily paper,
Solved a crossword clue, or read a book in bed.

I no longer walk the spaniel –
No! I read my BASIC manual,
If my son can understand it so can I.
Though my program isn't working
It is not because I'm shirking
It's because thus far I haven't found out why.

I've the LET instruction mastered,
But ON/GOTO has me plastered,
IF and THEN I only fight with if I must;
I find integers confusing,
Nested GOSUBs quite bemusing,
While FOR/NEXT loops leave me totally non-plussed.

My son treats me with charity,
He says that perfect clarity
Is difficult for withered brains to find.
I'll ignore his tittle-tattle!
I will not forsake this battle!
For good, or ill, I've BASIC on my mind!

Batch Communications

Batch communications are used when it is appropriate to gather together a batch of data in one location for transfer to another location.

Take as an example a chain of shops where individual stores submit sales information and stock replenishment requests to a central computer.

It would be possible to send details of each individual sale as it occurs, but it may not be necessary. All sales information can be collected into a consolidated batch for transmission at the end of the day, minimising costs and simplifying the job of the central computer.

This may sound like putting your entire batch of eggs into one basket. It is.

What do you do if the batch communications go wrong? Go home. The **operations department** is paid to worry about things like that.

Batch Processing

Some computer processes handle things individually, others handle things in batches.

An enquiry on a bank customer's current balance would be handled on an individual basis as and when required, for example because the customer has just walked into the branch and asked for it. The production of bank statements for all the branch's accounts, on the other hand, would be handled by a **batch processing** program or 'suite' of programs.

Batch processing, then, is the handling of data in batches by a suitable **application program,** or suite of programs. 'Suitable' excludes all those programs which are written to handle a batch of data every day but which take 25 hours to run.

Couldn't happen? Huh.

Baud

The **baud** rate is a measure of the speed at which data is transferred down a communications line.

Baud is pronounced as in 'The fact that absolutely no data has arrived down this line for the last seven hours does not **bode** well', not as in 'I'm getting **bored** stupid waiting for some data to come down this darned line'. The word originates from the name of one J. Baudot, a French telegraphic engineer who bit the dust in 1903.

Strictly speaking the baud rate is the number of times that the signal can change in a second, so if each change represents an on or off bit the baud rate is the same as the number of bits which can be communicated per second.

In fact baud rate is normally taken as being the exact equivalent of 'bits per second', or 'bps'. This is wrong. A signal which can be in one of four states after a change can convey the value of a pair of bits at a time, and the number of bits sent per second is then twice the baud rate.

Colloquially, though, '2400 baud' means 2400 bits per second, or 300 bytes per second. Small computers usually use speeds of up to 9600 bps when communicating with a central computer, or with their own local **peripherals.**

So if somebody refers to 2400 baud they almost certainly mean 2400 bps, but if you want to be sure you will have to ask them.

Of course, ***nobody*** likes a smart alec.

BCD

BCD stands for Binary Coded Decimal. See **packed data** for more information.

Binary

(Also see Supplements 1 & 2, pages 126-128)
Binary is a very famous and little understood system for handling numbers.

It is different from decimal in that it uses something called 'bits' rather than the digits 0 to 9.

As explained in the next definition, a bit is like an on/off switch. It can have two different values, 1 if on, or 0 if off.

A binary number is therefore represented by a series of bits set to 0 or 1, in the same way that a decimal number is represented by a series of digits set to 0 to 9. For example, the binary representation of the decimal number 217 is 11011001.

For more detail on binary arithmetic and conversion between binary and decimal see Supplements 1 & 2.

The two possible values of each element in a number is where the 'bin–' in binary comes from. Many computer people have worked on systems for years without having the first idea where the '–ary' comes from, so try not to worry about it.

Computers generally use binary arithmetic internally. If you want to know why, see bits.

Bits

A **bit** is about as low as you can get in a computer, unless you happen to be into slopes in electronic signals and that kind of stuff. This is why people who like to mess around with bits are called bit freaks, in much the same way that people who go underground caving are called complete idiots.

A bit is like an on/off switch, in that it can have one of two possible values, being 0 (off) or 1 (on).

The inside of a computer is infested with bits, which are used for just about everything. Some of the bits never change their value, and just sit there (see **ROM**). Some of them are changed quite a lot, for example by whatever is read in from a disk (see **RAM**). Some of them are rushing around from one part of the computer to another, for example from the keyboard to the screen while something is being typed in.

Some of the rushing around is done on things called **buses.** Any Reasonable Person knows that if you are in a hurry the last thing you do is get on a bus, but they go faster in computers.

So 'why use bits in a computer?' the Reasonable Person may well ask, particularly when everybody has been getting by with decimal 'digits' quite nicely for ages.

The answer is simply that it is a great deal easier for the Great **Chip** to think about millions of on/off switches than millions of electronic cog-wheels with ten positions on each.

Contemplating all those pretend cog-wheels whizzing around is enough to bring on effects normally associated with drinking a bottle of gin a little too fast.

So once you get rid of the cog-wheels with ten positions and substitute on/off switches with two positions you are stuck with bits whether you like it or not. The fact that this will subsequently confuse millions of Reasonable People is just the way it goes.

Meantime the computer goes on using combinations of bits for everything. For numbers (see **binary,** and Supplements 1 & 2), for letters (see **ASCII** for an example of making up letters from bits), and even for the programs themselves (see **object code** or **source code).**

Incidentally, the word 'bits' is derived from 'binary digits', which is why Computer People are often seen holding two fingers up in the air.

Bootstrap

The **bootstrap** is the resident program which gets a computer going after it has been turned on, for example calling in the **operating system** without which the computer is about as useful as a cuckoo clock without cogs.

The use of the word 'bootstrap' comes from the phrase 'pulling oneself up by one's bootstraps'. This describes the situation while a computer is being developed, when getting it actually started can be problematic. How can you load a start-up program into a computer which has not got started because it has not got a start-up program in it?

With difficulty. One method is to key in the program in **machine code,** one **semi-byte** at a time. Eventually enough is keyed in for the computer to be able to load further programs for itself. Hence 'pull oneself up by one's bootstraps'.

The bootstrap is in turn the origin of the phrase 'booting the computer'. This means to start up the computer, or give it a quick one with the right foot when nobody is looking.

Bubble Memory

A **bubble memory chip** holds data in the form of little magnetic 'bubbles', as opposed to the electronic signals used in a silicon chip.

If the power supply to a silicon chip is cut off all the signals, and thus the data, are lost. Bubble memory does not change when it loses power, so when you turn on again the data is still there.

This is clearly a good thing. So good that in the early 1980s bubble memory looked set to take over. The technology just needed a wee bit of tuning to get the right combination of speed of access, reliability and cheapness.

It's funny how long a wee bit of tuning takes.

Buffer

A **buffer** is an area of memory used for blocks of data which are on the move.

For example, you want to print a line on a printer. The line consists of various data **fields** which are scattered all over the computer memory.

When the print instruction is reached the systems **programs** will gather the data together in the buffer and then send it all to the printer in one go.

The characters will probably arrive quicker than the printer is capable of printing them. The printer therefore has its own buffer. It uses this to accept all the data from the computer, thus freeing the computer to get on with its next job. The printer can then transfer the data to the physical print head as soon as the head is ready.

It is hard to get excited about buffers.

For something slightly more exotic see **double buffering.**

Bug

Some Reasonable People think that once a program is working that is the end of the matter. Not so.

Some of the mistakes made in programs will in fact loiter under the surface for a while, then come and get you at some convenient moment, like 4.45pm on Christmas Eve.

This is how they got the name '**bug**'.

Different groups of people use various alternatives for the word bug:

Users	:	'A cock-up'
Systems Analyst	:	'Another cock-up'
Programming Team, in Public	:	'A Known Anomaly'
Programming Team, in Private	:	'A . . . (unprintable) . . .'

The reason bugs are able to loiter for so long is that they usually appear under peculiar, potentially untested, sets of circumstances.

Take as an example an error in a small company's payroll program:

1. The program checks whether an employee is paid weekly or monthly by checking an indicator in that person's record.
2. The indicator is set to 'W' for weekly or 'M' for monthly.
3. The error is that the program in fact checks the 3rd character of the person's first name instead of the 'W' or 'M' indicator.

4. Furthermore what the program actually does is check if it is set to 'M'. If it is not 'M' the program assumes it is 'W', being the only possible alternative.
5. The only employee of the company who is paid monthly is in fact the Office Manager.
6. The Office Manager is called Simon Greystone. The program therefore always treats him as monthly paid, because by pure chance the 3rd character of his first name is an 'M'.
7. As it happens no one else in the company has an 'M' in the 3rd character of their first name. The program therefore treats them all as weekly paid, because it assumes that anything which is not 'M' is 'W' for Weekly. This again is pure chance.
8. Some time the luck will run out and the bug will spring to life . . . And one December one Gemma Hardstaff duly joins the weekly-paid staff.

And on Christmas Eve, while the programmer is contemplating life from beneath a pink paper hat through the haze of seven pints of lager, an operator who for some reason is still working comes to Gemma Hardstaff and . . .

Bugger

This is the name given to a programmer who has put a **bug** in a program, and gave rise to the now common phrase 'You **bugger**'.

Bureau

A computer **bureau** hires out use ('time') on its own computers to customers.

Typical customers are those who are just starting to computerise, who wish to avoid a big capital outlay, who have an irregular pattern of work demanding occasional heavy computer use, or who wish to take advantage of a specialist service.

Bus

If a bit wants to move between a computer's central **processor (CPU)** and another internal component it will get on a **bus.**

The bus can be thought of as a set of connectors carrying bits around at terrific speeds.

The bus should always be there, so if you come across a bit waiting for a bus you had better tell it to try walking.

Bytes

A **byte** is a set of eight bits.

Strictly speaking a byte can comprise any number of consecutive bits, but only really old Computer People are aware of this.

A computer manipulates data in bits. This is okay for the computer since so long as it works things out correctly nobody is going to be too fussed as to how it does it, if it does it fast enough of course.

In fact it handles bits in groups, for convenience (see **processors).** Similarly anyone working with a computer or what it produces would find it hard going if everything was presented as strings of bits.

'What was that month-end figure again, Ron?'

'Zero.zero.one.one.zero.one.one.one.zero.one.zero.zero.one.zero.zero.one'

'Sorry, was that middle lot zero.one.one.zero or zero.one.one.one.?'

'Well, there was a zero.one.one.zero near the start . . .'

Bits and bytes have their place, which is preferably well out of sight.

To get back to the point. The first stage in converting the bit strings to handy things like letters and numbers is to put them into convenient groups. The most commonly used group consists of eight bits and is called a byte.

British Telecom wants to call bytes 'octets'. Quote: '. . . the precise term "octet" is preferred.' The fact that they are probably right does not mean we have to like their attitude.

The contents of a byte (the hell with octets) can be represented using something called **hexadecimal** to avoid all the one.zero.zero nonsense.

Eight bits can in fact be set up in 256 different combinations. Try it if you have nothing better to do. The first is 00000000 and the last is 11111111. 254 to go.

One piece of advice if you are going to do it; do not worry whether or not you are contributing to the progress of mankind. This sort of speculation will only slow you down.

Anyway, proven or not, you can take it from me that a byte can hold 256 different values, which gives loads of capacity for unique values for each letter, both lower and upper case, or small and capital if you prefer, plus all the odds and ends like numbers and punctuation characters. It still leaves other unique values for the computers to keep to themselves (see **control characters**).

A byte is therefore used as the basic unit for groups of bits; significantly it can thus hold one alphanumeric 'character', or two digits (see **semi-bytes**). The capacity of a computer's memory, or of storage devices like **floppy disks**, is also normally measured in bytes (also see **'K'** for Kilobytes, and **Megabytes**).

C

C is a high-level programming **language** developed with the **UNIX operating system**, the **systems programs** of which are actually written in C. Most operating system programs are written in a low-level **assembly language**.

C is therefore characterised by the needs of an operating system, for example providing facilities for dealing directly with the bits and bytes. It is also characterised by its name, which for descriptiveness and imagination matches its predecessor 'B'.

'What shall we call it then?'
'How about "C"?'
'That's a great idea.'
?

CAD/CAM

CAD/CAM stands for Computer Aided Design/Computer Aided Manufacture.

This is a pretty big area to be covered by just six letters. It includes robotics, production planning, quality control, draughting, modelling and design.

Programs to handle these functions need to be extremely sophisticated, as do the computers on which the programs run.

Take as an example a program which assists in the ergonomic design of a car seat. It has to process a lot of complex information on the human body, and needs to produce sophisticated displays and print-outs. This type of program has become practical through the use of advanced **hardware** and complementary **software tools.**

If you had tried to write such a program from scratch using only the computer systems available in the early 1970s it would have taken you an extremely long time. In fact before you had finished someone else would have used pencil and paper to design the seat, would have designed the rest of the car too, built it, filled it up with petrol and driven away in it.

CALL

CALL is included in the instruction set of several high-level **languages,** including **COBOL** and some versions of **BASIC.** It has the effect of summoning and executing a separate section of program, known as a program 'routine', after which processing returns to the statement after the CALL. The routine called may be a common routine used by a number of different programs, or a special routine written in a low-level language to do a particular job.

Low-level language routines are used for any jiggery-pokery which the high-level language is too unwieldy to do efficiently, if it could do it at all. The jiggery-pokery might be some bit or character manipulation, such as converting selected characters from lower to upper case, or direct access to **systems software** routines handling physical devices like the **floppy disk** drives.

You can get by for years without CALLing anything. A senior programmer on a mainframe system was asked to provide an example of the use of **assembler** routines called from a COBOL program. There was a long pause, then came the reply: 'Dunno'.

Cassette

A **cassette** is a cheap way of storing programs and data.

The use of cassettes is now restricted to home computers and just a few commercial applications. The reason for this is that cassettes are really only practical if you are happy to start at one end and work through to the other. As soon as you want to start hopping about looking for particular **records** you are in trouble. It just takes too long.

If your children have a home computer which can record programs on your cassette player, watch out.

'LET A=A+B: PRINT A' does not sound too good in the middle of a Brandenburg Concerto.

CCITT

The **CCITT** is the Consultative Committee on International Telegraphy and Telephony.

It is pronounced See-See-Eye-Tea-Tea. You should not attempt to pronounce it as just one syllable, particularly if you are on a crowded train.

The CCITT makes technical recommendations which are used as industry standards. For example, recommendation V24 takes the excitement out of a connection from a **modem** to a computer **terminal** by defining, amongst other things, which of the 25 wires the data should be arriving on.

Centronics Interface

The **Centronics** Data Computer Corporation makes printers.

At one stage they developed a particular type of **parallel interface** for connecting a printer to a computer. This interface somehow ended up as an industry standard.

Having a standardised interface means that a printer manufacturer can make a printer which can be plugged into all sorts of different computers. The standards cover the number and use of each of the connecting wires.

If your printer and computer do not have a common **interface** you have a problem. For a start the plug from one will not fit into the socket on the other. Overcoming this particular snag by some handiwork with a pair of pliers, a soldering iron, a hacksaw and some insulating tape may be fun but it will not get you anywhere.

Chad

See **punched cards.**

CHAIN

The **CHAIN** statement is included in some versions of **BASIC.** It ends execution of the program and specifies the name of the program to be executed next.

This means that the operator does not need to key in the name of the next program, which will be called in automatically.

This is useful in two types of situation:

1. Where it is a good idea to enforce the order of the programs to avoid the operator making a mistake. For example a CHAIN statement could be used to ensure that the program which sets all the company's accounting figures for the year to zero is executed ***after*** the program which prints them all out on the end-of-year report. This reduces the risk of the operator committing suicide.

2. Where a program is too big and has to be split into two or more parts. In the home-computer world CHAIN is most used by cheapskates who are too mean to buy that extra **RAM** pack, or who have frittered the money away on food, or clothes for the children.

Channel

Channels are the paths connecting different parts of a computer, for example the central unit and the various physical devices like the screen, keyboard, floppy disk drives or printer.

You could therefore have the printer on channel 1 and the disk drives on channel 2. You may even have the screen on channel 4 without having to sit through any adverts.

Check Digit

See **data validation.**

Check Point

See **restart.**

Chip

The great **chip** is just a chip off the silicon block.

The significance of the chip, or 'wafer', of silicon is that it is capable of holding an enormous amount of information in a very small area.

A chip the size of a thumb-nail can hold a hundred thousand **bits,** or on/off switches. The technologies which achieve this are called **LSI,** the Large-Scale Integration of electronic circuitry, or **VLSI** for Very Large-Scale Integration.

It is the extent of the chip's storage capacity, the speed with which it can be accessed, and the cheapness of manufacture which have revolutionised computer technology. Better a bag of chips than a warehouse full of valves.

There are alternatives to silicon, notably germanium arsenide. This raises the prospect of the Silicon Society being replaced by the Germanium Arsenide Society.

COBOL

COBOL stands for COmmon Business Oriented Language. It was first developed in 1959/1960.

It is a high-level **language,** and its instruction set is designed to make it easy to program commercial and accounting applications. If you wanted to write a program to work out the statistical significance of the results of five years of barnacle observation you would not use COBOL.

A COBOL program is split into four divisions:

- Identification
- Environment
- Data
- Procedure

If you want to discuss the merits of languages using divisions, and all you know about COBOL is what you have read here, you deserve everything that is coming to you.

COBOL has no causal connection with 'cobolling a program together'. This is an act of folly committed by somebody who is in too much of a hurry to think straight. 65% of programs which are cobbled together never work at all, 30% never work properly, and the other 5% take ten times longer to finish than was anticipated.

COMMON

COMMON is a statement in some versions of **BASIC** and in other languages which allows one program to leave data in memory for use by the next program. It does this by ensuring that when the next program is loaded it does not touch the common area of memory holding the preserved data.

COMMON is used in conjunction with **CHAIN.** It can be used to pass all sorts of data. The simplest example is the date. If you know that the operator would have had to key it in for the previous program it would be silly to ask for it to be keyed in again.

The common memory area is like common land in that all can use it but none can regard it as their own.

Compatibility

Compatibility deserves a special round of applause. It has made it into Computer Terminology without any significant distortion of its meaning.

Devices are compatible if they can work together. This can be by direct connection, such as a **peripheral** attached to a computer, or indirectly by physically transferring a disk or tape from one machine to another.

Of course you sometimes have to work at making things compatible, for example by making sure that any internal switches are correctly positioned. Having a computer sending 9,600 bits per second in **ASCII** to a printer which is expecting 300 bits per second in **EBCDIC** is like having 32 tennis players serving balls simultaneously to a goalkeeper who is expecting a penalty kick.

Always be cautious about compatibility. Remember Caan's Axiom:

'Compatible Tapes Aren't'.

Compiler

When a programmer sets pen to paper he has to use a programming language for what he writes. This is called the **source code** as it is this from which the program will be created.

Source code will vary from the English-like statements of high-level **languages** ('LET GROSS EQUAL NET+VAT') to the acronyms and mnemonics of an **assembly language** ('JNE' for Jump Not Equal).

The problem is that the central **processor,** or **CPU,** works at a very low level. It could no more understand what 'LET GROSS . . .' was asking it to do than could the average Copenhagen taxi driver decide where to go from instructions given by a visitor from Guatemala in his native tongue.

Help is needed, and it comes in the form of either the **compiler** or the **interpreter,** or even a little bit of both.

The compiler is a program which converts the source code into a compact form which the computer will be able to understand. This is called the executable, or **object code.**

A program is therefore written in source code, but when it is run on the computer it is only the object code which is needed. If you want to change the program you change the source code and re-compile it to get the new object-code version.

Of course a compiler has to look out for source code which does not make sense. When it finds an error it will print out a message for the programmer:

```
10 GOTO 33
*** ERROR *** How can I go to line 33 when there isn't one, stupid?
20 LET JOY
*** ERROR *** Let JOY what? Be unconfined?
30 GOOTO 80
*** ERROR *** "Gooto"?
40 GOTO 25
*** ERROR *** If I was you mate, I'd give up.
```

Computer

To compute is to calculate.

The original **computers** did just that. Calculate. In a room full of heavy-weight equipment with people employed full-time just changing the valves that had blown.

These days computers can not only calculate. Among other things they can control robots, aim missiles, direct spaceships, design all manner of other devices and let you play three-dimensional hyperspace ice hockey on your television screen.

You may or may not regard this as being a good thing. Personally I hate being beaten at three-dimensional hyperspace ice hockey by a six-year-old and I think that this clouds my judgement.

If you want to know more about computers have a browse through the rest of this book.

Configuration

These days computer installations consist of a set of physical units. These are the central control units plus supporting devices such as disk drives, printers, terminals and so forth. Even the central units of computers of the same range can come with different characteristics, say in the **memory size.**

The **configuration** is the complete installation, described in terms of the physical devices which comprise that installation.

A configuration may consist of a **mainframe** with 64 **Megabytes** of memory connected to 500 terminals with **on-line** disk capacity of 2,000 **Gigabytes.**

Another configuration could be your home computer with 16 **Kilobytes** of memory, plugged into a black-and-white Pye that cost £5 down at the market, and supported by on-line **storage** on a portable cassette player that your aunt found under your cousin's bed while doing the spring cleaning.

Constant

See **variable.**

Control Characters

The purpose of communication between computers is to transfer data.

Data is normally in the form of alphabetic and numeric characters, each being represented by a unique combination of bits such as are defined in the **ASCII** or **EBCDIC** character sets.

In order to make communications secure and efficient, computers also use combinations of bits which do not correspond directly to the sort of character you can see on a typewriter keyboard. These are called **control characters.**

A simplified example of the use of control characters is shown below. Computer A is trying to transfer some data to computer B.

The control characters being used are:

ENQ	Enquiry
ACK	Acknowledgement of receiving a message correctly
NAK	Negative acknowledgement. Distorted message received
WAK	Wait acknowledge. Not yet ready to receive the message
EOT	End of Transmission. No more messages

A	**B**	
ENQ⟶		Is anybody there?
	⟵ACK	Yes
Data1⟶		Here is a block of data for you
	⟵NAK	Sorry, didn't hear that clearly
Data1⟶		Here's the data again
	⟵ACK	Got it
Data2⟶		Here is another block of data
	⟵WAK	Hang about! I haven't sorted out the first one yet
Data2⟶		The second block again
	⟵ACK	Okay that time
EOT⟶		Goodbye
	⟵EOT	Goodbye

Control characters are also used to communicate with intelligent devices such as printers. The simplest examples are the line feed and carriage return characters. Many printers also accept 'Escape' sequences for more complex commands. The ESC control character is used to tell the printer that what follows is a command and is not for printing.

CHARS: LF–ESC–M–ESC–R–ESC–<–ESC–X–BEL–ESC–Z

HEX (ASCII): OA 1B 4D 1B 52 1B 3C 1B 58 07 1B 5A

TRANSLATION: 'Line feed/start bold print/start enlarged print/start double strike/start underlining characters/sound the buzzer/and turn yourself off'

Core

I have heard Computer People use **core** with three different intended meanings. These are:

1. Magnetic core **storage**: one of the earlier storage methods, using wires passing through a ring to induce changes in that ring's magnetisation. This is slow in comparison with electronic storage.
2. The User **RAM** (see **memory size**).
3. The part of the central **processor** which holds all sorts of stuff.

Definition 1 gets the prize for accuracy. Definition 2 was once true, in the days when the RAM was made of magnetisable rings; people who use 'core' for 'RAM' show their age. Definition 3 is used by people who are not entirely sure what they are talking about.

My personal reaction to Computer People who are not entirely sure what they are talking about depends on:

- whether I know what they are talking about any better than they do
- whether they have any say in the size of my end-of-year bonus.

CP/M

CP/M stands for Control Program/Monitor for Microprocessors. The popular view is that the 'M' stands for 'monitor', though a minority maintain that it in fact stands for 'microprocessors'. Stick with 'microprocessor'. Life is too short to worry about who is actually right.

CP/M is an **operating system** that provides programs running on microcomputers with easy access to and control of **files** on disks. It also provides a set of supporting features, for example for creating or transferring the files.

It was developed in the early 1970s by Dr Gary Kildall. He worked for Intel at the time, but this was an independent enterprise, and he reputedly did much of the work in his garage. I know of people who have tried to feed off this, for example by sitting in the garden hut to write a program for working out golf handicaps.

It has become a quasi-standard operating system, and programs running under CP/M on one microcomputer should be usable on another microcomputer which will also run CP/M.

Do not get carried away. If you write a program for a screen of 24 rows of 80 characters and try to run it on one which has 16 rows of 50 characters, do not expect any miracles.

There have been several significant lines of further development. One is CP/M-86, being a version for use on certain 16-bit processors. Another is

MP/M, for Multiprogramming CP/M, which provides for the simultaneous use of several terminals. Yet another is CCP/M, for Concurrent CP/M, which provides for the simultaneous running of up to four programs on a single-terminal computer. Which all goes to show what messing around in a garage can lead to.

CPU

The **CPU** is the Central Processing Unit of the computer. It is therefore fairly important.

The CPU comprises a number of specialised units. The most important of these is the program controller. Thinking of this as the conductor of the orchestra may help. On the other hand, it may not.

The program controller fetches the program instructions in the form of **machine code** from the memory (the size and potential power of the instruction depends on how many bits the processor can handle in one go, hence 8-bit, 16-bit and 32-bit computers). It then follows the instruction, for example by branching to another program location. If you decided to go along with the orchestra comparison, the program is the music score.

The controller may need to use other parts of the **processor,** for example the arithmetic unit when it is instructed to add two **fields** together, or the percussion section if it has reached the end of the 1812 Overture.

The CPU may also need to handle events which it has not instigated itself. They are called **interrupts,** and may come in the form of the pianist getting cramp, or a message arriving unexpectedly from another computer.

Occasionally the processor is asked to do the impossible, like call in the wind section of the Vienna String Quartet, or send some data to a non-existent **peripheral.** The CPU will then give up, sit down, and smoke a large cigar. This is called a 'Processor Check'.

CUG

CUG stands for Closed User Group. See **PSS.**

Cursor

The **cursor** is the marker on a screen which indicates the position which will be filled by the next character that the operator keys in. The curser is the operator who cannot get the cursor in the right place.

Daisy-Wheel Printer

A **daisy wheel** is a type of print head. It is used for both printers and typewriters to give a high quality of print.

The daisy wheel consists of a central hub from which emerges a complete circle of plastic spokes. Each spoke has a character on the end of it, like the characters on the arms of a conventional typewriter. When printing, the wheel spins in order to position the required character at the top, at which point a hammer pushes the character against the ribbon.

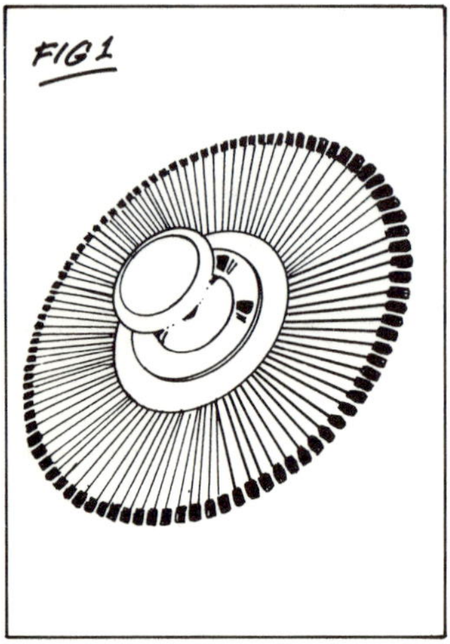

Life is pretty tough for these characters. When the printer is in use they are continually whipped backwards and forwards and round and round. In the pauses between movement they could be lying on their side or even upside down. The occasional pause in a completely upright position is accompanied by being smacked in the back by a hammer which forces their face into a ribbon impregnated with indelible ink on its way to being smashed against a rock-hard platen with a piece of paper wrapped round it. This is the sort of thing people pay money for at fun fairs.

Data

Data has been defined as 'facts given, from which others may be inferred'.

DP, or Data Processing, is all about inferring information from raw data. This covers everything from working out a payslip from the data of hours worked, tax rates, insurance rates and so forth through to deciding in which direction a rocket to Pluto should be pointed from information on the gravitational pull of Uranus etc. etc.

The English pronunciation of 'data' is as in 'skater', the American is as in 'starter'. If you want to say it 'datter' then I guess it doesn't matter but it's not professional chatter and I think you should be told.

Database

A **database** stores a whole load of data in one place, typically on disks of one variety or another.

Databases came about because modern computing is powerful enough to link together different applications.

Consider the sale of some goods. This could have resulted in an entry in the sales ledger and invoicing program, a separate entry in the stock movements program, another in the nominal ledger posting program and a fourth in the payroll program to record the salesman's commission.

This clearly is not efficient. Nowadays an integrated suite of programs could take the entry of the sale and do the rest automatically.

Once this type of thing happens it is not possible for each **application program** to have its own private **files.** The files too must be inter-linked. Enter stage right the database, which integrates the lot while letting each individual program get at the particular parts of the base which it needs for reading or updating data.

Controlling the data and access to it is so complicated that it has spawned a new abbreviation, DBMS, for DataBase Management System.

Working out what the DBMS was doing became so complicated that it in turn spawned a new job, the DBA, or DataBase Administrator. It is the DBA's job to stand in the middle of all the data that is rushing around and make sure that everything is proceeding smoothly. Directing traffic at the Arc de Triomphe is ideal experience for this.

Data Entry

Large volumes of data are usually entered into a computer system by specialist high-speed keyboard operators.

This type of operation is known as **data entry.** It is all about getting a mass of data into a computer as quickly and accurately as possible.

The accuracy is handled by different **data validation** techniques. Speed is maximised through the scientific design of the keyboard, the minimising of keystrokes required and the minimising of any delays to the operator while the computer performs supporting jobs like writing data away to disk. It will come as no surprise that the interests of accuracy and speed are usually opposed to each other.

The designers of data-entry programs put a lot of effort into getting the screen layouts right. A lot of this effort is wasted. Most operators never have the time or inclination actually to look at the screen.

Keyboards are not the only way of entering data into a computer, **bar code** readers, **OCR** readers and **MICR** readers being just three examples of the many alternative methods.

DATA/READ

See **READ**.

Data Validation

Data validation techniques are used to reduce the risk of error in operator entries.

The extent of data validation used is a vital criterion in the design of an **application program** or suite of programs. You can decide simply to check that alpha characters are not entered in **fields** that are supposed to be numeric. If this is inadequate, or if you've got any pride or ambition and want to move into the 20th century along with everyone else, you can add more complex validations such as those described below.

Check Digit:

The digits of, say, an account number are put into a formula from which an extra 'check' digit is derived. This is added to the end of the basic number, and stays there. When the whole number is entered the program can work out if the basic number is consistent with the check digit and, by signalling a keyboard error if it is not, eliminate a high percentage of keying errors. For example:

Basic number 81334 and a formula . . .

8+1+3+3+4=19 : Divide 19 by 10 :
Check digit = Remainder after division = 9
Complete account number = 813349
Therefore numbers 813340, 813341 up to 813348 **cannot** be valid.

If you think that you have never come across a check digit you are probably wrong. If you ever memorised your 14-digit bank sort code and account number, 2/14ths of your effort went into remembering check digits.

Hash Total:
This is a grand total of numeric fields, usually just amounts, previously worked out on a calculator or add list machine. Once an operator has entered the details of individual items on his micro he can enter the overall hash total. The program will then check that it is consistent with the total of the individual items.

Look Up:
Here the system looks up an existing data **record** to check information, say whether a stock number exists, and what type of stock it represents. This prevents operators in garages entering the sale of non-existent stock, or recording the sale of ten gallons of windscreen wipers.

Verification:
This is the re-keying of some or all of the data to check for consistency, eliminating a very high percentage of errors but obviously adding to total operator time considerably.

DBA

DBA stands for DataBase Administrator. See **database.**

DBMS

DBMS stands for DataBase Management System. See **database.**

Debugger

This is an **operating system** feature which is an aid to finding and removing any **bugs** in programs.

It is also used to describe a programmer looking for a bug in a program, often the same programmer who put it there in the first place. This is one reason why programming is such a strange job.

DIM

DIM is a **BASIC** statement which 'DIMensions' an area of memory ready for holding data. The area is called an 'array'.

The array consists of a number of data **fields** arranged in a 'matrix' of one or more dimensions. In a two-dimensional array, for example, each element is identified by two co-ordinates (X and Y). Take an array which has to hold the scores for 20 golfers for 4 rounds each. This would be set up as:

. . . DIM SCORES(20,4)

giving 20 sets of 4 scores, a total of 80 fields. To record the score of the 17th golfer in his 2nd round you use the statement:

. . . LET SCORES(17,2)=. . .

Some BASICs allow arrays of only one dimension while others allow two or even more. However big the array, it is clearly important to avoid trying to use a non-existent element, such as SCORES(22,2) in the example above. Nobody likes being told by a computer that their DIM isn't big enough.

Disk Cartridge

This is a **hard disk** platter in a rigid plastic case. It is the size of a very big frying pan.

A **disk cartridge** can be taken in and out of different disk drives, carried from one office to another, sent express delivery in an emergency, or left in an underground train after a good lunch.

Disk Pack

See **hard disk.**

Disks – General

Disks are used to hold data and programs. They provide convenient and quickly accessible storage. They can also be spelt 'discs'.

Disks come in different forms, such as **disk cartridges, floppy disks, hard disks** and **Winchester disks,** but the principle of operation is always the same.

The surface of a disk holds data in magnetic fields. It is divided into a pattern of sectors and tracks, which the computer uses to identify the area of the disk it wishes to read from or write to.

Fig. 2 shows a 'stack' of disks, where it is necessary to identify a location by surface as well as track and sector numbers. In this case each track forms a cylindrical shape through the stack, and is therefore sometimes called a 'cylinder'.

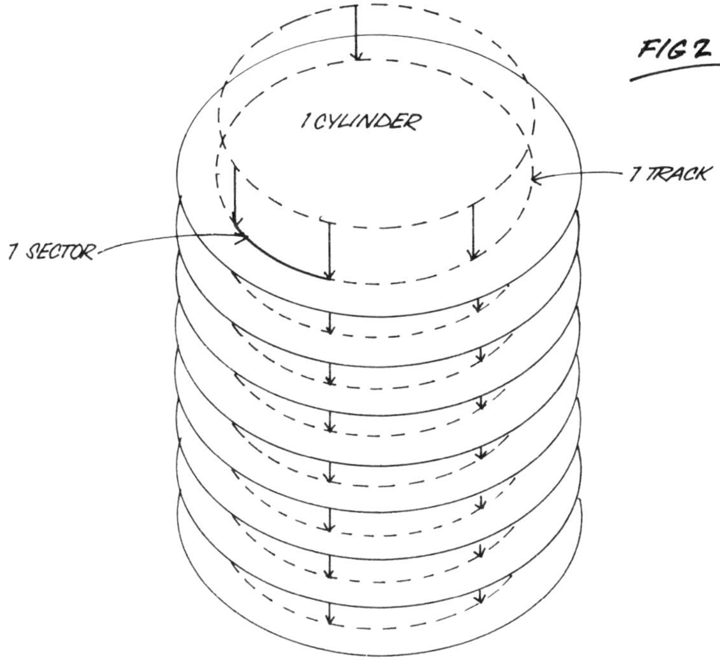

FIG 2

When the disk unit receives an instruction to read a particular part of the disk it positions the magnetic 'head' to the correct track. In the meantime the disk is whizzing around at an amazing speed (some drives spin continually, others only when actually accessed). When the right sector comes around the head reads the data and transfers it to the computer's central unit.

From this it is clear that the total access time comprises the data transfer stage and the 'latency' period in which the head is positioned and then waits for the right sector to come rushing by. Generally speaking the latency period is rather longer than the transfer time.

Sometimes a malfunction leads to the head bouncing round on the disk. This does not do either the head or the disk much good, as anybody who has sent the stylus hopping across his favourite track on an LP will appreciate.

The computer version of this is called a 'head crash'. If you have a problem reading a disk cartridge it may have been caused by anything from a minute particle of dust that was passing through to a full-scale head crash. If it was a head crash it may have been the fault of the disk, or it may have been the fault of the disk drive device.

You can test for this by putting the disk cartridge into another drive. If the heads on that drive crash too, suspect the disk. You can test the original heads by putting a good disk into that drive. If they screw up the good disk it was probably them to blame in the first place. To be sure, check them with another disk that you know is okay. You should also test the original disk on another drive. When you run out of disks and drives, call an engineer.

Distributed Processing

The 'classic' large computer system consisted of a **mainframe** computer connected to 'dumb' **terminals.**

The terminals are considered to be dumb (American for 'stupid') because they are completely controlled by the **application program** on the mainframe, and have no **software** or data **storage** capacity such as is provided by disks.

In this situation the processing is said to be centralised because all the programs are running on the central computer. It makes no difference if the terminals are all in the same central location, or scattered all over the country, or both.

The advent of cheaper microcomputers has made it possible to spread this burden of work, by replacing the dumb terminals with 'intelligent' terminals. These have their own storage capacity, typically on disk, from which local programs are loaded and on which data can be stored.

Intelligent terminals can do part of the processing locally, for example the **data validation,** thus providing **'distributed processing'.** This avoids the delays and costs incurred by the frequent transfer of information between the mainframe and a dumb terminal. It also means that the terminal can carry on even if the mainframe, or the connection to it, should fail.

If you are writing a program for a **network** of intelligent terminals you do so in the knowledge that eventually hundreds of operators will be using that program all over the country.

Under these circumstances the phrase '. . . but the operator will never do that . . .' ceases to have any meaning. Whatever 'that' is, an operator will do it. I know. So be careful. Watch out. Keep your wits about you, and when you go to bed each night try to think of the thing you've probably forgotten.

Dot-Matrix Printer

A **dot-matrix printer** is inexpensive and prints relatively quickly, typically at around 100 characters per second.

The print head consists of a block, or 'matrix', of needles. Each character is formed by the selection of an appropriate set of needles, rather like electronic scoreboards which use individual lights to make up a number to be displayed.

As the print head moves sideways the different combinations rush in and out, smacking the ribbon against the paper to leave patterns of dots representing different characters.

Double Buffering

Double buffering is used to speed things up by reducing the time which has to be spent waiting for physical processes such as reading from a disk or printing on a printer.

Say you want to read a series of **records** from a disk and print each one.

If your program only uses one **buffer** it will have to:

1. Start the read of a record into the buffer
2. Wait for this operation to finish
3. Start the printing from the buffer
4. Wait for the printing to finish

The buffer is now free for the next read

Go to step 1 for the next read.

This is like driving at 25mph.

If you are the sort of person who likes to cook a meal, do the ironing, finish a crossword and watch television at the same time, read on. This is how a double bufferer would go about it:

INITIAL Start read of record 1 into buffer A
Wait for the read to finish

1. Start print from buffer A AND
   Start read of next record into buffer B, which is free.
   By using different buffers the physical disk reading and printing operations are happening at the same time, saving time.
2. Wait for print from buffer A and read into buffer B to complete.
3. Start print from buffer B, which now has the data from the last read AND
   Start the read of the next record into buffer A, which is now free again.
4. Wait for both operations to complete
   Go back to step 1.

And so it can go on, 'flip-flopping' between the buffers.

This is what is known as double buffering. In some situations you can even gain from treble or quadruple buffering. If your program is for printing out the telephone numbers of the members of the rugby club, quadruple buffering would be a slight overkill. Still, getting it working correctly would keep you busy for a year or two.

Dual Processor

Many **mainframe** computers use two processors to improve performance. Also see **FTS** for Fault Tolerant Systems.

EAROM

EAROM stands for Electrically Alterable **ROM.** See **PROM.**

EBCDIC

EBCDIC is a coding system which defines the combinations of 8 bits which represent each character and **control character.** It is IBM's version of **ASCII.**

If you want to mention EBCDIC in conversation pronounce it either Ebb-Sid-Ick or Ebb-Ked-Ick.

Incidentally, it stands for either Every Bloody Character Definitively and Incontrovertibly Coded or Extended Binary-Coded-Decimal Interchange Code, depending on how technical you want to be.

EEROM

EEROM stands for Electrically Erasable **ROM.** See **PROM.**

EFT

EFT is either a small newt or an acronym for Electronic Funds Transfer.

It is usually possible to determine which from the context. However if you overhear somebody saying 'I've had it up to here with efts' you had better keep an open mind.

A small newt is a small newt. Electronic Funds Transfer is all about moving money using computerised electronic communications rather than postbags full of cheques, paying-in slips and the like.

When you take fifty pounds out of an Automatic Teller Machine an EFT would be used to deduct the money from your account.

END

The word '**END**' crops up in a number of programming languages. It does not take a genius to work out that it means that the end of something or other has been reached.

The 'IF END . . .' statement in **BASIC** tells the processor which instruction to go to if the program tries to **read** or **write** beyond the end of the **file.** For example the following statements would make the program branch to statement 3000 if file number 3 turns out to be too small:

```
10    IF END #3 THEN 3000
      . . . .
      . . . .
3000  PRINT "BUY A BIGGER DISK, SKINFLINT"
3010  STOP
```

EPROM

EPROM stands for Erasable Programmable **ROM.** See **PROM.**

Error

There are two major types of error in the computer world.

The first type is an error in a program. See **bug.**

All other errors are the fault of the systems analyst. Systems analysts do not mind getting blamed for errors: they are used to it, and it is what they get paid for. For more detail, see **systems analyst.**

Escape Sequence

See **control characters.**

Fallback

Fallback and Recovery tend to hang around together, usually in the gloomy part of the **systems specification** which describes what happens if something goes wrong, like a **hardware** failure.

Their meanings are quite different. If your car breaks down while you are on your way to your aunt's the fallback is getting a bus. This lets you carry on, albeit not so quickly. The recovery is calling out a garage, getting the car fixed, collecting the car and generally getting yourself back to where you started from.

If an **intelligent terminal** is connected to a **mainframe** and a worker puts a pick-axe through the line connecting the two, the fallback would be to carry on working **off-line,** that is without access to the mainframe's **files.** If the same worker then puts a pick-axe through the local power cable the operator has to retreat to the next level of fallback. The first thing to be done here is to sharpen a pencil.

FDM

FDM stands for Frequency Division Multiplexing. See **multiplexing.**

Feasibility Study

Contrary to popular conjecture the Computer Person does occasionally try to work out in advance whether a **project** is actually feasible. This attempt is called a **feasibility study.**

A lot of the excitement of working on a project stems from wondering whether it will actually work, and in this respect a good feasibility study is a bit of a dampener.

In fact feasibility studies do not do much for ***la joie de vivre,*** though reading one in retrospect can be a good laugh.

Field

A discrete unit of data, such as an amount or an account number, is referred to as a **field.**

This is not the same thing as a magnetic field, though data can of course be held in series of magnetic fields on **storage** media such as disks or tapes. Fields can also exist in the computer's memory while a program is running.

In a generation's time children will wonder how the word for a unit of data came to be used to describe a plot of ground with cows standing around in it.

File

An individual unit of data such as an account number or balance amount is held in a **field.**

An associated group of fields, such as 'account details', is stored as a **record.**

An associated group of records, such as 'all deposit accounts', is held in a **file.**

These days it is a bit non-U to have only files. Anybody who is anybody keeps data in a **database.**

Firmware

Firmware lives in the twilight world between the **hardware** and the **software.** It is usually a low-level program (see **languages**) for doing something very complicated.

It is called firmware because it is so complicated that nobody can decide whether it should be burnt into a **chip,** thus becoming hardware, or kept as software so it can be changed easily the next time it goes wrong.

Firmware comes into the category of 'things most Computer People cannot understand', and is therefore scornfully left to the bit-freaks. The Normal Computer Person only refers to firmware in sentences like 'They've probably changed the ****** firmware'.

Flag

Computer programs use **flag** characters or bits to retain information which is not simply alpha or numeric data. They can take on any specified value, the simplest being 'Y' or 'N' for Yes or No, to indicate whether a particular event has occurred.

Flags may be used purely in memory while the program is running, or saved as part of a data **record.**

Flags in records carry supplementary information, for example to indicate whether the manager had to give his authority for a transaction to proceed, say cashing a cheque for a customer who is already overdrawn.

Memory flags are usually an indication of which route a program has taken. For example a program which allows you to display or modify a record may change a flag from 'N' to 'Y' if you do actually modify a **field.** If the flag is still set to 'N' when you finish, the program does not need to bother to re-write the record.

As any marathon runner will tell you, you can expect to flag a bit, but when you start to flag a lot you are in real trouble.

Floppy Disk

A **floppy disk** is literally that, a thin floppy disk coated with a magnetic surface. It is encased in an 'envelope' for protection, the surface being accessed through a slot cut in each side.

Floppy disks provide a reasonably reliable and quickly accessible storage medium at a low price, and as such are an essential element in the advance of the microcomputer. The capacity of a disk would normally be somewhere between 100 **Kilobytes** and 1 **Megabyte.**

My favourite example of computer packaging is the box of floppy disks which boldly announces on the front 'Flexible Disks' and warns, on the back, 'Do not bend'.

Flowchart

A **flowchart** is a diagrammatic representation of a flow of processing. It shows the different possible routes that a program or suite of programs could take, and the criteria for selecting each route.

Systems analysts and programmers use flowcharts to give a clearer view of what a system or individual program should be doing than is possible with just the written word.

The example below shows the use of two of the standard flowchart symbols, the process box and the decision box. It is presented with apologies to devotees of **structured programming.**

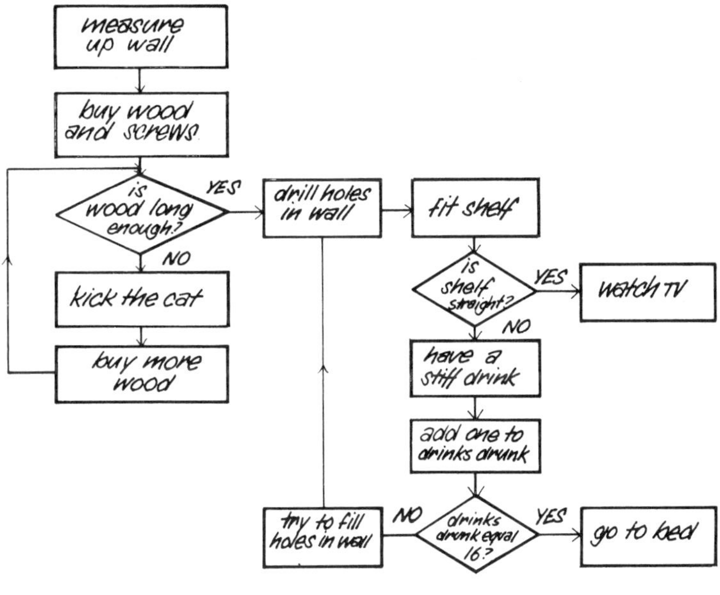

FOR/NEXT

The **FOR/NEXT** instructions, in **BASIC** and other languages, make the computer repeat a process a defined number of times.

The FOR statement defines the number of times that the repetition will occur; it does this by setting 'start' and 'finish' values for any **variable** you choose.

The NEXT statement increments the variable after each repetition. The program keeps 'looping' until the variable reaches the 'finish' value.

In the example below the variable is 'Numbereaten', and 1 and 28 are the start and finish values respectively.

10 Open a box of mint chocolates
20 FOR Numbereaten equals 1 to 28
30 Eat another mint chocolate
40 NEXT Numbereaten
50 Swear never to eat another mint chocolate again

The NEXT in statement 40 has the effect of returning the program to statement 20, until the variable 'Numbereaten' has reached its finish value of 28. The program will then carry on to statement 50.

FORTH

The **FORTH** language was designed for use on micro- and minicomputers. It was developed by Charles Moore and Elizabeth Rather at the US National Radio Astronomy Observatory in the early 1970s. Make of this what you will.

FORTH uses a data 'stack', which comes from the back of the **RAM** forwards, and a 'dictionary' of program words which goes from the front of the memory backwards, hopefully not meeting the stack somewhere in the middle.

FORTH programs leave **BASIC** programs standing for speed. They could also be considered easier to write, but only in the way that it is easier to dig a big hole with an excavator than a shovel. First you have to know how to use the excavator.

FORTRAN

FORTRAN is a high-level **language** with an instruction set designed specifically for scientific applications.

Writing a sales ledger program in FORTRAN would be about as sensible as using **COBOL** to find the co-efficients of the polynomial which best fits a particular set of data.

FORTRAN stands for FORmula TRANslation. It was developed for the IBM 704 computer in the 1950s and has since become widely used. Between 1957 and 1962 Fortran I, II and IV made it into the outside world. Fortran III did not. I do not know what happened to Fortran III, and those who do would probably prefer not to discuss it.

FTS

FTS stands for Fault Tolerant System.

An FTS can tolerate **hardware** faults because it has two of everything. Furthermore it uses both sets all the time, so if a component fails nothing is lost, and nothing has to stop while the replacement is fitted.

This virtual elimination of a whole range of hardware failures can lead to significant savings in systems analysis and programming time, most of which is expended on handling protection against hardware failures and operator madness.

Eliminating operator madness may prove the more difficult.

Functionality

Functionality is a useful word with an ugly sound.

I mean, how can anyone feel the full joy of a host of golden daffodils with words like 'functionality' kicking around in the back of his mind?

Anyway, it is used to describe *what* a computer system does for its users, as opposed to *how* it does it.

Users can get pretty annoyed if a Computer Person messes around with their functionality without telling them first.

Functional Specification

See **specifications.**

Function Key

See **keyboard.**

Gate

A **gate** is a part of a processing **chip** which can be open, partially open or closed. When open it allows signals to pass through, when partially open it allows selected signals to pass through, and when closed it allows nothing to pass through.

This sort of gate cannot be jumped over and is no good for leaning on.

GET

GET is a program instruction in many languages. It instructs the computer to go and GET a data record from a **storage** unit such as a disk or magnetic tape.

Some languages use **READ** instead of GET, and the fact that some **BASICs** include GET and some do not typifies the lack of standardisation.

Indeed some languages, again including some versions of BASIC, have both GET and READ instructions. They will have slightly different meanings, varying from language to language, and even a Computer Person has to ignore his better instincts and reach for a manual.

Gigabyte

A **gigabyte** is a gigantic number of bytes:

1 Kilobyte **(K)**	=	1024 BYTES (approx 1 thousand)
1 **Megabyte** (M)	=	1024^2 BYTES (approx 1 million)
1 **Gigabyte** (G)	=	1024^3 BYTES (approx 1 American billion)
1 **Terabyte** (T)	=	1024^4 BYTES (approx 1 British billion)

Gigo

The grand old principle of all computing:

'Garbage In, Garbage Out'.

Glitch

See **redundancy check.**

GOSUB/RETURN

GOSUB is a **BASIC** instruction that branches the program into a **subroutine.** The

RETURN statement is at the end of the subroutine and branches the program back whence it came, to just after the GOSUB.

Subroutines are used to ensure a disciplined program structure. They are also used for sections of program which are needed repeatedly. Making such a section a subroutine avoids the need to keep repeating its program instructions; they are included only in the subroutine, and are accessed by a GOSUB whenever needed.

For example, a programmer may want to use a routine that displays "Confirm? Press Y for Yes or N for No," and allows the entry of 'Y' or 'N' only, at the end of every screen. This would be included as a subroutine.

Another example is how I proceed when looking after the house:

```
10    Get newspaper from front door
20    GOSUB 2000
30    Check if cat's water bowl is empty
40    If water bowl is empty, fill it up
50    GOSUB 2000
60    Phone someone for a chat
70    GOSUB 2000
      etc . . .
      etc . . .
2000  Make cup of coffee
2010  Read newspaper
2020  Drink cup of coffee
2030  Eat biscuit
2040  Eat another biscuit
2050  Decide what to do next
2060  RETURN
```

GOTO

The instruction **GOTO** results in a sudden leap from one part of the program to another.

This is like travelling in hyperspace, in that you go from one place to another without being anywhere in particular in between.

If you ever wondered why GOTO's are supposed to be incompatible with **structured programming**, just draw a **flowchart** of a program based on hyperspace journeys.

Hard Coded

See **READ**.

Hard Copy

See **printers**.

Hard Disk

Hard disk is a term for rigid disks, differentiating them from **floppy disks.** Like a floppy disk, however, the hard disk has a surface coated in magnetic material, and is used for the **storage** of data and **software.**

A hard disk unit may incorporate a number of 'platters' in a stack, or it may have only a single platter. In either case the unit may be permanently fixed in a disk drive, or may be of the type that can be moved from one drive to another.

The most common type of fixed disk for small computers is a sealed unit called the 'Winchester Disk'. The movable variety are normally called 'Disk Packs' in the case of stacks of platters or **disk cartridges** for single platters. Storage capacity can go from a cartridge of five **megabytes** to a pack of several hundred megabytes.

Hard disks are more hard-wearing than floppy disks, they have far greater storage capacity, and they provide much quicker transfer of data. They also cost a lot more.

Hardware

Computer **hardware** describes the physical units of an installation.

If you can stand a cup of coffee on it, or sellotape a cartoon to the side of it, it is probably hardware.

Hash Total

See **data validation.**

Head Crash

See **disks–general.**

Help Screen

A **help screen** provides help to a computer operator who is not sure how to use a program, or who would just like an answer to the classic question 'How do I get out of this?'

The help comes in the form of supplementary information of the kind that traditionally was written in a manual and thereafter ignored completely.

Hexadecimal

This is derived from the phrase 'What the heck's a decimal number doing mixed up with all these cursed bits'. It is a system for describing the contents of a **semi-byte** conveniently.

A semi-byte consists of four bits. Its contents could be described as 0000 or 0001 or 1101 or whatever value they happen to hold, but this would obviously become very tedious. **Hexadecimal** notation allows a semi-byte to be described in a single character.

As a semi-byte can hold values from 0 (0000) to 15 (1111) the decimal numbers 0 to 9 are insufficient. They are therefore supplemented with A (=10) up to F (=15). Hexadecimal numbers therefore go from 0 to F.

The 16 possible values of 0 to F provide an alternative derivation of the word 'hexadecimal', because Hex represents 6 and Decimal represents 10, at least they do if you're Greek.

A byte, being a pair of semi-bytes, can then be represented by a pair of hexadecimal numbers. It can thus take the values from 00 (0000-0000) to FF (1111-1111).

High-Level Language

See **languages.**

Home Computers

Home computers are **personal computers** bought for use in the home. While they must therefore be suitable for playing computer games, they can also be used for **applications programs** such as a personal accounts program.

Home computers can often stimulate conversation, most frequently along the lines of:

'Can you think of anything useful that I can do with this darned thing?'

Housekeeping

Computer systems need **housekeeping** in the same way that houses do. Sometimes the housekeeping is essential, and sometimes it just pretties things up a bit.

Computer housekeeping usually involves the **files** of data. Designing a system to capture all the data you want can be extremely complicated, but it is often child's play compared with working out how to get rid of the darned stuff when you have finished with it. Getting rid of unwanted data and tidying up what is left is housekeeping.

Take as an example a file of account **records.** When a new account is opened a new record is added to the end of the file. When an existing account is closed the simplest thing to do is to set its account number **field** in the record to O's but leave the record there (this is called a 'logical', as opposed to 'physical', deletion). All accounts with number 0 can then be ignored.

There is one clear snag in this. The file is getting longer. The only compensation is that it is also getting 'holes' in it where the logically deleted records are.

These holes are no actual use unless a housekeeping program 'compacts' the file, getting all the live records to the front of the file by physically over-writing the logically deleted records, that is, getting rid of the holes.

This is pretty much like washing up, where you can carry on without doing any for a while but eventually reach a point where it is essential, unless you resort to eating out all the time.

IF/THEN/ELSE

The **IF/THEN/ELSE** statement is common to a number of high-level **languages,** including **BASIC** and **COBOL.**

Its function is to re-direct the program if a specified condition applies. IF the condition applies THEN the program branches to a different address. In many languages it is not actually necessary for the programmer to include the word 'THEN' in the statement.

The ELSE is an optional extra which gives the programmer more room for manoeuvre, or enough rope to hang himself, depending on how you look at it. It is not available in many versions of BASIC, probably because of many BASIC programmers' proneness to accidental suicide.

The example below shows IF/THEN/ELSE being used in combination with **GOSUB** by somebody singing 'Ten green bottles'. This example is something of an experiment in computer education. We may never know the results of the experiment, which is probably just as well.

Why not have a glass of sherry?

Right, here we go.

```
10    LET NUMBERLEFT=11
12    REM Start at eleven as one is subtracted immediately
20    LET NUMBERLEFT=NUMBERLEFT-1
```

```
30   REM Reduce number of bottles left by 1
40   IF NUMBERLEFT=0 THEN 60 ELSE GOSUB 2000
50   REM If they've all gone then get the hell out of here
55   REM but if there are any left do a bit of singing
58   GOTO 20
60   STOP
70   REM End of program
2000 Sing "There are NUMBERLEFT green bottles hanging on the wall
           NUMBERLEFT green bottles hanging on the wall
           And if one green bottle should accidentally fall
           There'll be (NUMBERLEFT minus 1) green bottles
           Hanging on the wall."
2010 RETURN
```

Implementation

The **implementation** of a computer system is its first step into the real world of real data and real operators.

Anybody with a nervous temperament, which includes everybody with experience of implementing computer systems, will have tried to reduce the excitement by first having a **parallel run.**

Implementation means different things to different people:

Project Manager:
He thanks anyone with whom he is still on speaking terms. He adds the name of the project to his CV.

Systems Analysts:
The systems analysts usually try to change jobs before anything they designed is actually implemented. If they have not succeeded in doing this they get ready to get the blame.

Programmers:
They look forward confidently to bug-free program running, and will say things like 'I'm going on holiday' and, later, 'Is that ***still*** working?'

Trainers:
The trainers know what went on during operator training and are consequently more nervous than anyone else.

Operators:
They keep making mistakes. Fortunately all of these mistakes can be blamed

on the project manager, systems analysts, programmers and trainers. For a while, anyway.

User Department Management:
This varies.

Data Processing Manager:
He mumbles ridiculous things to his staff like 'Makes it all worthwhile, don't you think?'

Ink-Jet Printer

See **printers.**

Input

In order to produce anything, a computer program must have some materials to work with, as does any manufacturing process.

A program's equivalent of raw materials and components is referred to as **input.** It comes in the form of data. The data may be entered through a keyboard, read from a **storage** device, or even sent by another computer. The end product is called **output.**

Input often comes from a combination of different sources. A program which prints invoices may receive all sales details through the keyboard but get the customer's name and address from a disk file.

Large computer systems may separate original input and final output in

time and space. For example, the sales information input by a data-entry operator at a remote location may only be output as part of a centrally produced report for the sales manager.

Anyone who plays fruit machines will recognise the operator's situation in this sort of system. You put a lot in and get precious little out. To make matters worse, you know that somebody somewhere is putting precious little in and getting a lot out.

Instruction Set

A program gets a computer to do something by giving it **instructions.** Of course the instructions have to be in a form that the computer can understand, and this is done by writing them in accordance with the rules of a programming language, that is by use of the language's **instruction set.** The instructions are also referred to as 'statements'.

Given below are the six main categories of instructions from the **COBOL** language, which cover everything except the screen and keyboard handling. This grouping could be applied to most languages used for commercial applications, though specialist languages, such as those for handling graphic design, may have a slightly different make-up.

1.	Arithmetic:	Add, Multiply, Divide ....
2.	Data Manipulation:	Move, Transform ....
3.	Input/Output:	Open, Close, Read, Write ....
4.	Procedure Branching:	Go To, Alter, Perform ....
5.	Conditional Branching:	If, At End ....
6.	Special Features:	Debugging aids, report generation ....

Integer

An **integer** is a whole number. It has no fractions or decimal places.

Many versions of **BASIC** allow the programmer to specify that a number will always remain an integer by including a '%' at the end of the **variable** name. For example 'NUMBER%' rather than just 'NUMBER'.

Why bother?

Well, if the BASIC **interpreter** knows in advance that the number that it is about to process does not have any monkey business like decimal places it can process it more quickly. It can also store it in a smaller number of bytes, which is particularly useful if it forms part of a **record** on a disk where you are trying to keep the records as small as possible.

In fact most BASICs store integers in a 2-byte **field.** This can hold up to 65,536 different values (from **hexadecimal** 0000 to FFFF). This is why integers are usually allowed values in the mysterious range −32,768 to +32,767.

Intelligent Terminals

See **terminals.**

Interactive Communication

Interactive communication between computers allows one to respond directly to a message received from another.

This type of question-and-answer communication is required where the operator of a **terminal** needs information from a remote computer immediately. Examples of this are information on whether an item is available from stock, or on the current balance in a customer's bank account.

This question-and-answer connection is the computer equivalent of talking on the phone, as opposed to sending a letter.

Using a communications line throughout the day, and having a central computer ready to deal with central enquiries as they occur, is an expensive business. Installation of an interactive **network** is therefore usually preceded by a cost/benefit analysis. Here the manager first decides what he wants to do and then gets his staff to produce a report justifying the decision.

Interface

Computer installations are totally reliant on the different parts of the system interacting with each other.

The different parts may be **hardware,** like the **CPU,** the **peripherals** or even separate computers. The connection between them is called the **interface.** It is what allows them to interact.

The interface may concern only data messages, as in the case of messages being passed between an **application program** and the **systems software.** However, it can also involve the swapping of electronic signals, such as between a computer and a printer, or a computer and a **modem,** or even between one modem and another. These days the screen and keyboard are said to provide the 'operator interface'.

Use of a word can go too far.

I once attended a telecommunications seminar where the presenter was trying to tell the audience to ask questions as they cropped up: He did this by saying:

'We want to maximise the, er, interactivity of the, er, interface here today so if you, er, have a question just, er, flag an interrupt'.

Having been brought up on ***Winnie The Pooh*** makes it very difficult for me to handle this sort of thing.

Interpreter

A program is written using the instruction set of a programming language. What the programmer writes is called the **source code** of the program.

The instructions can vary from the English-like statements of a high-level **language** to the acronyms and mnemonics of **assembly languages.** The problem is that none of them make any sense to the computer's **processor,** which can only handle **machine code.**

One way to bridge the gap is to convert the code before the program is run (see **compiler** for details). Another possibility is to interpret the source code at **run-time.**

The **interpreter,** sometimes called the run-time interpreter, does just this. It is a program which tells the computer what to do by interpreting the source code. It is simple and convenient but not very efficient; generally speaking it is better to make the conversion effort only once with a compiler than interpret it every time it runs.

My first experience of interpreters was not a happy one. It occurred when I was making up the numbers at a buffet reception for foreign bankers. It was not the interpreter's fault, it was mine. I have since had some bad experiences with computer interpreters, but nothing to match this.

Anyway, I prefer not to think about it. It still makes my forehead go red.

Interrupt

Whilst a computer is running a program it may occasionally have to divert its attention to deal with an outside event that has just occurred.

The outside event is called an **interrupt** because it interrupts the normal flow of processing. It may be something quite innocent, like an enquiry message being received from a remote computer. Alternatively it may be bad news, like the electronic signals from a printer going haywire because it has just had a cup of coffee spilt into it, or the **CPU** protesting that it has just been asked to divide a gallon of petrol by the name of a breed of dog.

Anyone who has received an urgent telephone call in the middle of a meeting will know that interrupts are more often bad news than good. As a former manager of mine once said into a phone, 'What did you drive into THAT for? I only just painted it!'

I/O

I/O stands for **Input/Output.**

The I/O is what it is all about. A computer system which did not output anything would be no use to anyone, and a system which had nothing put in to it would be unlikely to output anything.

The I/O handling is one of the trickier things to sort out in a program. This is because a number of possible results have to be catered for. If a program tries to read a **record** from a disk it has to know what to do if a message comes back saying that the disk drive appears to be on fire.

If a programmer confesses to having a bit of trouble with his I/O, do not be embarrassed.

Jackson, Michael

See **structured programming.**

JCL

JCL stands for Job Control Language.

JCLs came into being because many **batch processing** jobs are too complex to be achieved by a single **application program,** and therefore have to be done by a series, or 'suite', of programs. On a **mainframe** it would be nothing unusual to need 20 programs to do one job.

These would be run as a linked series, quite probably overnight. The running order of the series needs to be set up in advance, as does information for each of the programs, such as which **files** it will be using and where they are located. Setting this up in advance reduces the risk of error, and lets the late-shift operator eat his take-away chinese in relative peace.

This type of job control is achieved through use of a Job Control Language. The example below uses IBM DOS/JCL, but many microcomputer **operating systems** have similar, though simpler, job-control facilities. In the example 'comment' lines are indicated by an asterisk.

```
// JOB STAT L123M
*  JOB TO PRODUCE MONTHLY STATEMENTS
// ASSIGN SYS020, X 'TO2'
// TLBL SYS020, 'STAT.MAST'
*  USE FILE STAT. MAST ON TAPE DRIVE TO2
// ASSIGN SYS030, X'DO2'
// DLBL SYS030, 'STAT.EXTRACT'
// EXTENT SYS030,1,0,100,500
*  SET UP AND USE FILE STAT.EXTRACT ON DISK DO2
// EXEC EXT
*  RUN PROGRAM 'EXT'
// .....
```

My first contact with this particular JCL occurred in bed at two o'clock in the morning. I heard my wife saying, to a harrassed shift operator who had just phoned up, something like '. . . well we'll have to use a tape then. Try taking out the SYS030 DLBL and use a slash–slash–TLBL–X–apostrophe–zero–two . . .' Sweet dreams.

K

K stands for Kilobyte. However, this does not mean 1000 bytes, it means 1024.

This is because 1024 is a handy number in **binary,** where it is expressed as 100000000.

The computer-press advertisements for jobs have started to quote salaries in K's. This means that very few people in the computer industry know what they will be earning when they start a job.

Key

When a program gets a **record** from a **file** it has to indicate which one it wants. You could deliberately write a program which gets records like prizes from a bran tub, but would only want to if you are a complete idiot.

Sometimes the program just wants the next record, say when processing a file of banking transactions. On other occasions it wants a specific record, such as the data for a particular bank account. In the latter situation it specifies the record that it wants by the record's **key,** in this case the account number.

Some systems allow primary and secondary keys, say the account number as primary and the account holder's name as secondary, for use if the account holder has forgotten his number. Others even allow whole ranges of 'major' and 'minor' keys, for example to cater for people who have also forgotten their names.

A key is also the name for the plastic things on the keyboard that you poke with your fingers.

Keyboard

The **keyboard** is the most common means of entering data into a computer.

It can comprise just about any combination of normal typewriter keyboard, a numeric keyboard for easy entry of purely numeric data, a group of keys for controlling the screen and the **cursor,** and a set of 'function' or 'program' keys.

The function keys are used for easy selections. For example a theatre box-office system may have keys for the ticket sales function, for enquiries, for cancellations and for advance bookings. These allow the operators quickly to indicate which of the program's functions they require.

It has been demonstrated that the pattern in which the normal typewriter keyboard is arranged does not make a lot of difference to a practised typist. However, most computer users are definitely not practised typists.

The standard QWERTY pattern was originally adopted because it ***separates*** letters which frequently occur together. This helped prevent adjacent arms of the first mechanical typewriters from getting caught up with each other. It could reasonably be supposed that this scattering of letters slows down the average computer user.

Oh joy, oh bliss! Zillions of quid to speed things up and a keyboard to slow you down.

Key Punch Operator

See **punched cards.**

KILL

KILL is a **BASIC** statement. It is used to KILL a disk **file,** that is to delete it from a disk.

'Kill' seems a bit melodramatic for just erasing a file. One manual goes even further by explaining 'kill' with reference to files that have been 'eliminated' or even 'expunged'. Still, if a file has got to go it has got to go, and there is no point in being sentimental about it.

BASIC being BASIC, only some versions include KILL.

LAN

LAN stands for **Local Area Network.**

Languages

A program instructs a computer what to do. It gets the computer to understand the instructions by using a pre-defined **language.** The language provides a set of words, or 'keywords', which have a valid meaning; anything else masquerading as an instruction is rejected.

Languages vary considerably in their format and the style of programming that they demand. They also tend to be oriented towards a particular use through the range of instructions that they make available to the programmer.

Languages fall into one of three general categories. These are high-level languages, low-level languages, and **BASIC.**

A **low-level language** is so called because it has a set of instructions for handling everything at a very low level, manipulating bit patterns and dealing with data **fields** one or two bytes at a time. The instructions are usually acronyms or mnemonics (e.g. ADC for Add with Carry and SRL for Shift Right Logical from the Z80 assembly language).

In a **high-level language** the instructions can handle whole data fields, or multiple branching decisions, which would take a series of instructions in a low-level language. This makes it a lot easier to get the program working correctly, saving expensive programmer time. A high-level language normally has instructions which are close to the English language (e.g. MOVE and **IF/THEN/ELSE).**

BASIC is BASIC. It can be thought of as a high-level language, but just thinking of it as BASIC avoids confusion.

LET

LET is a common high-level **language** statement that forces a variable to assume a new value. The fact that 'let' sounds voluntary, or even permissive, is misleading. The only voluntary thing about it is that some languages do not actually insist on the word 'LET' being included (see below).

LET can be simple:

LET A=B (or just A=B)
LET A=A+1
LET DESCRIPTION$="CRATE OF PEANUTS"

or complex:

LET A=(((((B*C)/D)*E)/F-TAN(H))+(D*E)/(D*COS(H))+27/C)

If you can understand the complex example, I suggest that you quit reading this book and go and do something useful.

Listing

See **program listing.**

Local Area Network

It has been estimated that 75% of all written and spoken office communications are purely internal to an organisation. Of these internal messages 75% again travel less than 600 feet.

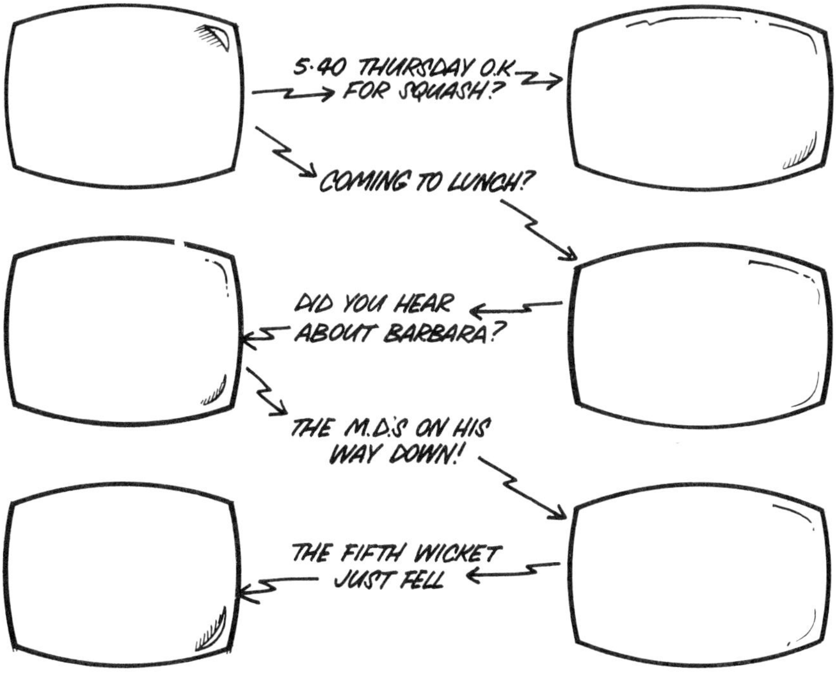

Enter the **local area network,** or LAN. This is a system for carrying local communications between all manner of devices. The devices can be computers, computer **terminals** or other devices such as printers, measuring instruments and so forth.

This type of **network** allows the exchange of information. It also facilitates the sharing of devices like high-speed printers or disk drives. A LAN may support anything from three to a thousand or more devices; calling two connected devices a network is done by the same people who call a **file** a **database.**

Look Up

See **data validation.**

Loop

Programmers use **loops** to avoid repeating sets of program instructions.

A program which has to calculate the VAT charges for a series of sales would loop round a set of instructions, performing one loop for each sale. The instructions in the loop would fetch the next 'net' amount, multiply it by the VAT rate, and store the result.

Program loops are okay if you can get out of them, but a **bug** which traps you in a loop is definitely bad news. Apart from anything else it may take quite a while to find out where you are actually stuck.

If a Computer Person says, in any context, 'I've been through this loop before' he means 'I've been in this situation before and ended up going round in circles'.

Low-Level Language

See **languages.**

LSI

LSI stands for the Large-Scale Integration of electronic circuitry.

It is this technology which allows loads of information to be crammed onto a **chip.**

You may also come across references to VLSI, being Very Large-Scale Integration. Roll on ELSI for Extremely Large-Scale Integration.

Machine Code

A computer **processor** acts in response to program instructions. The instructions which the processor is able to handle itself are patterns of bits referred to as **machine code.**

These days the instructions are first written in a programming language and then converted to machine code by a **compiler** or **assembler.** In the good old days it was often necessary actually to write programs in the old machine code, particularly on small computers.

There were all sorts of weird and wonderful ways to feed this code into the machine. One small computer took its programs from a drum in which a set of tiny red plastic combs was loaded. Each comb started out with eight prongs, and thus represented one byte of 8 'on' bits. The programmer worked out the bit pattern that was required for the machine code of his program. He then took a set of combs and snapped off the prongs in positions where he needed 'off' bits before placing the combs in the drum.

You could tell when someone had been programming one of these machines because of all the bits of red plastic in their hair. Those were the days.

It is easy to understand why Computer People with experience of this sort of machine-code programming consider themselves to be a breed apart from those who write things like 'LET TOTAL=AMOUNT1+AMOUNT2'.

Macro Instructions

Some **assembly languages** offer a facility to make life easier for the programmer who has to repeat a particular set of instructions in different places in a program.

The facility is called the **macro instruction.** It is included in the program along with the normal instructions from the language's instruction set. The **assembler** then converts the macro into a pre-determined group of normal instructions. This saves the programmer repeating the writing of the group of instructions, and thus reduces the chances of error.

The programmer determines what the set of generated instructions will be when he sets up the macro. It can have **operands,** and these are used as operands for the generated instructions.

Very occasionally a programmer gets addicted to setting up macros. He will gradually lose sight of what it was that he originally set out to program. He will start to work evenings and weekends writing bigger and better macros. He may even stop drinking. There is no known cure for this condition.

Magnetic Media

Magnetic media is the general term for anything which stores computer data on a magnetised surface. **Disks, magnetic tapes** and **cassettes** are the most commonly used magnetic media.

Although a 'magnetic medium' may have supernatural connotations, references to bleeding disks are strictly earthbound.

Magnetic Tape

Magnetic tape provides a physically compact but high-capacity storage medium. It is usually an acetate tape coated with a magnetised surface.

The main shortcoming of tape as a storage medium is that it is not practical for use by a program which will need to access the data randomly. Winding and re-winding simply takes too long, and disks are much better for this type of application.

Computer rooms in cinema films usually have more than their fair share of magnetic-tape machines, whereas in the real world there is a preponderance of disk drives, for the reasons mentioned above. The misrepresentation occurs because tapes stuttering backwards and forwards look terrifically technical. Watching the outside of a disk drive in action is about as exciting as watching the outside of a fridge.

Mainframe

The **mainframe** was the framework of the central unit of early computers. The **processor** and associated units were mounted on this.

The frameworks are long gone but the word 'mainframe' lingers on. At the moment it means a very big computer.

Major Key

See **key**.

Megabyte

This is not a great big byte. A byte is a byte and that is that.

A **Megabyte** is in fact a great many bytes. A kilobyte is 1024 bytes (see '**K**'), and a megabyte is 1024^2 bytes in its turn.

Memory

The computer's **memory** is where it holds programs and data. The memory is physically held in one or more **chips**, in the form of millions of electronic 'on/off' switches known as **bits**.

Some memory is 'volatile', in that it can be changed by programs, and its contents are lost when the power is turned off. This type of memory is called **RAM**, or Random Access Memory.

Some memory has fixed contents which never change and which are not lost when the power is turned off. This is called **ROM**, or Read Only Memory.

Memory Size

A computer's quoted **memory size** is the size of the **RAM**. The contents of the **ROM** are the fixed intelligence of the computer and are not included. Usually.

A '64K micro' is therefore a microcomputer with a 64K RAM (see **K** and **RAM**). Large computers have memories holding many **megabytes**.

The RAM is used because this holds the **application programs** and the associated data, and is therefore of most relevance to the user. In fact it may also hold various odds and ends as well (see **systems programs**), and what is left over is sometimes referred to as the 'User Ram'. The User RAM is thus the memory available for the User's own application programs and data.

Unfortunately knowing the size of the RAM, or even how much of it is User RAM, does not necessarily tell you whether it will be big enough to run the application programs that you want it to run. Consider the following:

A 64K RAM will hold	64	Kilobytes
	= 64 × 1024	Bytes
	= 64 × 1024 × 8	Bits
	= 64 × 1024 × 8	On/Off Switches
	= 524,288	On/Off Switches

In other words a 64K User RAM makes 524,288 on/off switches available for the application program and data. If a Reasonable Person wants to know how much he can expect to be able to do with 524,288 on/off switches he can ask a Computer Person.

If you do this just bear in mind how you normally react yourself to ridiculous questions.

Menu

A **menu** is a means of allowing a computer user to make a selection from the available options.

A menu displays a brief description of each option, usually alongside a number. Entry of the appropriate number tells the program which option is required, for example:

1. Create New Records
2. Amend or Update Records
3. Delete Records
4. Print Records
5. End Program

The system of computer menus using numbers came about because the dedicated Computer Person eats only Chinese take-aways, and is thus under the impression that 'A seven, a twenty-eight and a sixty-three' is the norm for indicating menu selections.

Merge

Some microcomputers have a **'merge'** facility, which allows the 'merging' of program statements from a cassette tape with the statements of a program already held in the memory. A real Computer Person only merges files. See **sort.**

Methodology

This means 'approach'. It is derived from the cumbersome old English word 'method'.

It entered the computer world because a Computer Person realised that two years was one hell of a long time to spend working out an approach to a problem, but was not very long for constructing a **methodology.**

MICR

MICR stands for Magnetic Ink Character Recognition. The most common use of magnetic ink is on the bottom line of bank cheques, where it is used for printing the account number, sort code and cheque number.

The value of the system is that it allows both humans and computers to read the same set of characters. This is achieved by mixing lumps of metal in with loads of ink and using the ink to print with. Humans can read by seeing the ink, and an MICR reader on a computer can read by first magnetising the ink and then detecting the pattern of magnetised particles.

Microcomputer

A **microcomputer,** or 'micro', is a small computer built round a **microprocessor.** The term is generally used to include the keyboard, screen and other devices such as **floppy disks.**

When a micro gets big enough it becomes a mini. Nobody knows how big this is. Many a marketing man has pondered on whether it is better to have a big micro or a small mini.

Microprocessor

A **microprocessor** is a central processing unit **(CPU)** squeezed onto a very small **chip.** Its functions are the same as those of larger CPUs.

It is interesting to compare a modern microprocessor-based computer with one of the very first computers, ENIAC (for Electronic Numerical Integrator and Calculator) which was completed in 1946. The microprocessor is about 0.001% of the weight, uses about 0.002% of the power and is more than 15 times faster.

The capabilities, cheapness, compactness and reliability of the microprocessor put it at the heart of the current computer revolution. If you wanted to run a program in your sitting-room with a reconstructed ENIAC you would have to accommodate, among other things, some 1,800 valves.

Microsecond

See **millisecond.**

Millisecond

The power of today's computers means that one hell of a lot can happen in a second.

In order to avoid senior programmers having to say things like 'Can't you get that to happen any faster than one four-hundred-and-twelve-thousand-seven-hundred-and-twenty-fifth of a second?' the second is frequently split into smaller time units:

1 **Millisecond** = 10^{-3} seconds (1 thousandth)
1 Microsecond = 10^{-6} seconds (1 millionth)
1 Nanosecond = 10^{-9} seconds (1 American billionth)
1 Picosecond = 10^{-12} seconds (1 British billionth)

Minicomputer

A **minicomputer,** or 'mini', is a computer which is bigger than a microcomputer but smaller than a **mainframe.**

If you do not think that this is precise enough to enable you to tell, for example, whether a largish computer is a mainframe or a mini do not worry. Nobody else can tell either.

Minor Key

See **key.**

MIPS

MIPS stands for Million Instructions Per Second, which is one indication of the power of a computer's central **processor.**

The instructions referred to are the low-level **machine-code** instructions that the processor handles directly. It may take hundreds of these to execute a complex high-level **language** statement.

A **mainframe** may run at 10, 20, 30 MIPS or more, whereas micro-computers typically do not aspire to even a single MIPS. If you boasted that you had a fifth of a MIPS micro it is unlikely that anyone would have the faintest idea what you were on about.

Modem

Modem stands for MOdulator/DEModulator. It is the name of the box of electronic wizardry that enables computers to communicate with each other over ordinary telephone lines.

The box of wizardry is necessary because signals go in and out of computers as a series of on/off bits ('digital' signals), whereas the telephone network is designed to carry the wave patterns of voice communications ('analogue' signals). Modems are used in pairs, one to MOdulate from digital to analogue at the transmitting computer end, the other to DEModulate back to digital form at the receiving end.

Networks which are designed to carry digital signals all the way are much more efficient for computer-to-computer communication. These networks are increasing in number.

The Computer Person wants to use these digital networks for as many purposes as possible. Naturally one of the first things to consider is how you can use them for carrying voices . . .

See also **acoustic coupler.**

Modular Programs

Some development systems allow programs to be constructed as a series of separate modules, as opposed to a single lump of code.

One great advantage of this type of **modular program** is that the introduction of one small change does not necessitate the re-compilation of the entire program (see **compiler).** The programmer needs only to re-compile the affected module and 'link' it back in with the others.

This avoids a lot of idle time during re-compilation. It is bad news for writers of non-modular programs who are in the custom of using the time to go shopping or to sink a couple of pints. In order to be compatible with single-module compilation times hobbies must be suitable for activity periods of just a few minutes. Knitting is the obvious choice.

There is another type of modular programming whereby the program is structured into separate modules 'logically' although it is physically stored and compiled as one unit. Many modern languages enforce this type of programming.

Mouse

A **mouse** is a device which makes it easy for an operator to 'point' at a particular item on a screen.

The mouse itself is a small box on castors. When the operator rolls it around on a flat surface an indicator, or **cursor,** is moved around the screen. The screen displays the options available to the operator, who can indicate which is required by positioning the cursor next to it through use of the mouse, then pressing a button on the mouse.

This sort of development is a mystery to the traditional Computer Person, who regards rolling a little box around as completely idiotic, especially when all the operator would have had to do otherwise is key in something obvious like '>RUN PR/COM/PAR7:'. Anyway, the traditional Computer Person prefers to use the flat surfaces near his own terminal for the storage of the listings of all the programs that he has written since joining the organisation.

Multiplexing

Multiplexing is a technique for using one wire to provide several different and separate communications channels simultaneously, just as if they each had a wire of their own.

This saves a lot of wire. Saving wire is no big deal of course. Saving laying it is though, and multiplexing allows increased use of existing connections.

The two commonest techniques for multiplexing are time division (TDM) and frequency division (FDM). The former works by letting each of the channels in turn have use of the wire for a tiny time 'slot'. The latter allocates each channel its own frequency range from the overall bandwidth. In both cases the net result is one high-speed line being used as several lower-speed lines.

Multiplexing is achieved by a **hardware** device called a Multiplexer, or MUX for short. There is no need to be offended if you hear a Computer Person talking about shoving something through a MUX.

Multiprogramming

Multiprogramming is a technique which enables a single **processor** to run several **application programs** simultaneously.

The technique was developed because a processor can go a lot faster than the outside units that it is attached to. It would be crazy to have a processor that can handle 20 million instructions per second sitting with its feet up while a lone operator is keying in characters at the rate of 5 per second.

In a multiprogramming system the application programs held in different 'partitions' of the computer's memory take it in turn to have a 'slice' of the processor's time. During its time slice the program proceeds normally; at other times it is suspended.

The time slices are measured in **milliseconds.** The suspension periods between time slices are therefore not noticeable. The programs thus appear to be running simultaneously, though they are in fact being run on a rota basis.

Some systems actually dump entire programs onto disk for the suspension time slices, and use the memory for something else. See **virtual** for more information.

Multiprogramming techniques have spread from the larger computers down to many microcomputer **operating systems.** If you are a computer hobbyist who is looking for new challenges after savouring the nuances of the **FOR/NEXT** instruction you could consider having a go at knocking up a small multiprogramming operating system.

MUX

See **multiplexing.**

Nanosecond

See **millisecond.**

Network

A **network** is a series of inter-connected points. A computer network, or 'net' to the cognoscenti, is a series of inter-connected computers.

The pattern of inter-connections varies according to the type of network. The only sort of net that any of them look like is a fishing net after a losing battle with a swordfish.

One of the most glamorous-sounding jobs in the computer industry is Network Controller, carrying as it does images of a seat of power behind an enormous console of switches, dials and flashing lights. The image is sometimes accurate, but if you go for an interview for a job as network controller it would be as well to check if you have to supply your own screwdrivers.

NIT

NIT stands for Non-Intelligent Terminal. See **terminal.**

Number Crunching

The Computer Person refers to large-scale arithmetic calculation as **number crunching.**

Remarkably, there are many Computer People who can say 'Number Crunching' without looking embarrassed.

Object Code

When a programmer writes a program he is writing the **source code.** He uses the instructions of a language, where the instructions could be the English-like words of a high-level **language** or the acronyms of a low-level language.

The source code is good for the programmer but not for the **processor,** which is not designed to spend all day wading through the English language.

In order to make life easy for both the programmer and processor, **compilers** and **assemblers** are used to convert the source code into what is known as **object code.** This could be **machine code** for the processor to execute directly, or could be an 'intermediate' code which works with the help of an **interpreter.**

Object code is totally incomprehensible to all but the processor or interpreter, or the bit-freak programmer who likes to go messing around with it.

In truth, a bit freak will go messing around with object code whether he understands it or not.

A direct change, or 'patch', to the object code does cut out all the trouble of re-compiling a program in order to introduce a modification. It also makes life interesting for someone else who has to modify the program later, and makes the horrifying discovery that the source code does not correspond to the object code. The knowledge that the original programmer made a mental note of what he changed in the object code does not provide much consolation.

OCR

OCR stands for Optical Character Recognition. This is a technique that enables a computer to read the same set of characters that is recognised by a human.

OCR relies on characters being printed in a particular form. The reader device is able to recognise the shape and thus transfer the appropriate character into the computer.

The readers do not work very well on a bit of paper which has spent several days in the back pocket of Nick the Builder, has had an outline house extension design sketched across it and has seen temporary service as a beer mat. OCR is more likely to be used on controllable bits of paper, such as gas meter readings, with the more robust **MICR** being used for more worldly items like cheques.

Octet

See **byte.**

OEM

OEM stands for Original Equipment Manufacturer.

The term came into existence through the widespread practice of one computer company marketing **hardware** produced by another, often adding value in the form of software **packages** or other hardware components.

You may think that the OEM is the original manufacturer of the equipment.

Remember, this is the computer industry. Believe it or not, the OEM is actually the company that buys from the manufacturers, adds value, and sells the resultant packaged product.

OEMs often put their own brand name on the hardware. This practice can make the question 'Who made this stupid thing anyway?' very hard to answer.

Off-Line

See **on-line.**

ON/GOTO

Arriving at an **'ON'** instruction in a **BASIC** program is like arrriving at a roundabout, in that one direction has to be selected from the several which are available.

ON works by using the value of a **variable** to indicate which direction is required. If the value is 1 the first direction is taken, if 2 the second, and so forth.

In the example below the variable is 'Numberofchildren' and has a value of 1, 2 or 3. The possible directions are program statements 50, 60 and 70.

```
 10 ON Numberofchildren GOTO 50,60,70
 50 Buy 1 lollipop:  GOTO 100
 60 Buy 2 lollipops: GOTO 100
 70 Buy 3 lollipops: GOTO 100
100 Relax for five minutes
```

ON can also be used in combination with **GOSUBs** instead of **GOTOs.**

On-Line

A computer is said to be **on-line** when it has a live connection to another computer and off-line when it does not.

An **intelligent terminal** is said to be on-line when it has a live connection to a computer and off-line when it does not.

A dumb terminal is said to be on-line when it has a live connection to a computer and completely useless when it does not.

Operand

A program instruction tells the computer **processor** which operation to perform. The **operand** associated with the instruction tells the processor what to perform the operation on.

In the **assembly language** instruction 'ADD A, B', 'ADD' is the instruction, and 'A' and 'B' are the operands. In this case the result of the operation is held in 'A', which some would therefore call the destination operand with 'B' as the source operand.

Most program bugs stem from operand trouble. This is not surprising. It would take some kind of oddball to write:
'LET RATE=((AZ*20)+((BZ-2)/10)*(AZ-7)+BZ)/100' and get the 'LET' wrong.

Operating System

An **operating system** is the **software** which makes it possible to run **application programs.**

The operating system will handle tasks such as the allocation of memory, the loading of programs and **overlays,** the **input** and **output** of data and the simultaneous running of several programs. It also provides **utility programs,** such as those for copying disks, copying **files** or sorting files into a particular order.

The more powerful the computer, the more sophisticated the operating system is liable to be, including specialities such as **Virtual** Memory Management or **Network** Control.

When programmers were programmers the smaller computers did not have operating systems, programs being written in **machine code** or similar. Indeed it is curious to recall that I became a Software Consultant before knowing what an operating system was. In fairness to myself it should be said that I had already embarked on a large-scale self-education exercise. I was probably one of the only software consultants in history to keep a copy of 'Data Processing Made Simple' in his briefcase.

Operational Specification

See **specification.**

Operations Department

The **systems analyst** defines what a suite of programs should do. The programmer writes the programs. It is then the job of the **operations department** to put the system into operation.

All the operations department, or 'ops', has to do is change disk packs and tapes, load the right sort of paper onto the printers, and fix anything that goes wrong.

This is obviously a piece of cake.

Some people in ops claim that there is more to the job than meets the eye. Big deal. What meets the eye may well be the night-shift operator listening to Dire Straits and eating his way through a take-away Chicken Tikka Masala with Bombay Aloo. Between mouthfuls he may explain that:

- a failure may lead to the corruption of live data, on disk or tape or in memory.
- the **hardware** which may fail is dotted around the country from Lands End to John O'Groats.
- retrieving vital data stranded in Warrington by a telephone-exchange failure in Reading is no simple matter.
- programmers do not like being telephoned at 3.30 in the morning with perfectly reasonable enquiries.

Some people are always moaning.

Output

There are two classic approaches to designing a computer system.

The first approach involves analysing the requirements of the system, starting with the **output.** The output is addressed first because the whole point in having a computer system is to output something useful. Output could be a print of a bridge design, a screen full of information on the current status of a bank account, navigational instructions for transmission to an aeroplane, a printed report on the company accounts or a set of printed payroll slips, to take a very small group of examples.

The second classic approach to designing a computer system is to start by writing the program and see how things shape up as you go along.

A computer system which does not output anything useful is called a Mistake.

Overlay

Many programs are bigger than the available memory.

The obvious solution is for the programmer to persuade the appropriate authority to buy a bigger computer. The authority may be the programmer's wife, husband, mother, father or Data Processing Manager.

In the quite likely event that the appropriate authority prefers to spend the money on a new armchair or a new set of filing cabinets the programmer has to resort to **overlays.** These are sections of the program which are only called into memory when they are going to be used, instead of being resident all the time. Certain areas of memory are then used for whichever overlay is required at any one time.

Packages

Packages are programs written in such a way that they can be run by users with different requirements. The 'personalisation' of the package program is achieved by a user setting up his own set of information as to how it should run. This set is often called the **parameters.**

Packages came about because the computer industry eventually realised that it was not very efficient to have thousands of people continually re-writing virtually identical programs.

Now there are thousands of people continually re-writing virtually identical packages.

Packed Data

Generally it is a good thing to hold data in as compact a form as is practical. This can save space in a computer's memory or on disk or tape, and can reduce the cost of sending data over communications lines.

Data is normally held in an 'unpacked' form in which each character occupies the 8 bits of a byte. The 256 possible combinations of bit values provide more than enough for a unique definition of each upper-case letter, lower-case letter, numeric digit and punctuation mark.

If you know in advance that a character is going to be a numeric digit of 0 to 9 then you only need 4 bits to define it uniquely. Numbers held in 4-bit groups, or **semi-bytes,** are referred to as **packed data** or binary coded decimal (BCD).

Of course to be able to pack data you have to be certain that it is entirely numeric, as it is the four chopped-off bits which would have distinguished between the number and the different characters. For example in **ASCII** code '5' would be indistinguishable from '%', 'E', 'U', 'e' or 'u' without the first four bits.

Packing data is therefore okay for telephone numbers but not for the house number which usually occupies the first characters of the first address line. It would only need someone to call their house 'Dun Roamin' and the system would get completely confused.

The sentiment that if people will call their houses 'Dun Roamin' there is nothing much that anyone can do is understandable, but does not solve the problem.

Packet Switching

Packet switching is a type of communications system.

Computers communicating with each other in this way wrap blocks of data up in 'packets' and send the packets into a general **network.** The network uses addressing information on the front of the packet to ensure delivery to the right computer.

A packet-switching system is able to send packets along different routes, thus smoothing out congestion in particular sections or avoiding any sections where a failure has occurred. This flexibility provides a better service than the traditional method of using a fixed and dedicated **channel** all the way from one computer to another.

Packet switching is sometimes referred to as 'X25'. This is because the standard definition of the **interface** between the network and a computer using it is the **CCITT** Recommendation Number X25.

A system has to be extremely sophisticated to handle the millions of packets whizzing through it. The designers of such a system would never get started if they had any tendency towards pessimism. They need to be optimistic, but extremely cautious. In fact paranoid optimism is an essential characteristic of a network designer.

PAD

PAD stands for Packet Assembly/Disassembly Device. See **PSS.**

Paper Tape

Paper tape is a cheap and cheerful medium for storing data.

Its most common use nowadays is on telex machines, where a message is keyed in and recorded on the tape, which can then be re-read for the message to be transmitted. This avoids the cost of keeping the telex line open during the keying-in.

The bit pattern recorded on the tape corresponds exactly to the bit pattern sent down the line, and a standard code is obviously needed for defining what is represented by each pattern of bits.

The international standard code used for telegraphy, and thus for the paper tape on telex machines, is called **CCITT** Alphabet No. 1. It is also called Baudot code, although it was created by a Mr Murray. Mr Baudot did create a code himself. This is CCITT Alphabet No. 2. It is not hard to imagine how Mr Murray feels, inventing an international standard and having it named after the wrong bloke.

Standard telex tape has 5 columns in which holes can be punched, though 6, 7 and 8 column tape is still in use in some computer installations. Coding systems define the pattern of holes and non-holes which represent each character.

When paper tape has been used once it is useful for throwing off sky-scrapers.

Parallel Interface

A **parallel interface** allows a set of bits to move from one place to another in parallel, each bit moving along a separate **channel**.

This is different from a **serial interface** in which the bits move along a single channel one after another. The parallel interface is potentially quicker, but it is more complex to handle.

Peripherals such as printers may be connected by either type of interface. Parallel interfaces need a lot of wires for the data bits, plus a few wires for control signals. Serial interfaces have two wires for the data bits (one for each direction) and lots for control signals. There must be a great deal of money in wire.

Parallel Run

When a computer is introduced it is usual to start by running it in parallel with the previous system in order to verify that the new system is producing the correct results. This is called the **parallel run.**

This is a bad time for everyone. The management are nervous. The user department have to adjust to the system while still running the previous one. The analysts and programmers who have worked hard on the system for months now have to wait around doing nothing just in case something goes wrong . . .

They told me at school that programming was fun,
But nobody mentioned the parallel run . . .

My program worked perfectly well for a week
While I sat in a corner all modest and meek,
Looking calm on the outside, not saying a lot,
While my insides were tied in a petrified knot.

But by Friday I felt I could start to relax
And stopped bracing myself for the nervous attacks,
And by late afternoon I was feeling all right,
For the week had gone well, not an error in sight.

As I put on my coat I was singing a song
When I heard the dread words 'I think something's gone wrong!' . . .

It is midnight, I'm tired, confused and depressed,
I can't find the bug though I have done my best
The branch manager's waiting to finish his work
And the analyst's told him he thinks I'm a jerk
My boss says it's clear that my lessons aren't learnt
While my wife rang to say that the dinner is burnt
The security guard wants to go as it's late
And I'm trying and trying to keep my thoughts straight . . .

Oh! They told me at school that programming was fun
But nobody mentioned the parallel run . . .

Parameters

Parameters are a set of data which determine how a program will run. They mean that one program can run in a variety of ways; this avoids the need to modify the program itself to cater for every variation. It also means that variations can be introduced by a user without the need for a programmer.

For example the parameters for a very simple payroll program might consist of:

Monthly or Weekly Payslips?
Number of overtime rates (1 or 2)?
Overtime Rate 1 (e.g. Base rate×1.5)?
Overtime Rate 2 (e.g. Base rate×2)?
Private Pension Scheme? . . . etc.

The word 'parameters' is also used in a general way by the Computer Person, as in 'Give me the parameters on that one, John.'

This sort of comment should be met with the response, 'What on earth are you talking about?'

Parity Bit

A **parity bit** is a simple way of checking whether a set of bits that have travelled along a line have arrived intact.

It works like this. The sending computer takes the set of bits representing a character and adds up the number which are set to 'on'. It then adds the 'parity' bit, setting it to 'on' or 'off' as required to ensure that the group as a whole has an even number of 'on' bits (this is even parity; odd parity works in a similar but opposite fashion and is just as common). The receiving device will then check that each group has an even number of 'on' bits. If it has, then the character is accepted and the parity bit thrown away. Otherwise the character is rejected.

So you want to know what happens if two bits get distorted, thus introducing a compensatory error? Look, it may be necessary to play the clever clogs to get anywhere with computers, but do not expect anyone to like you.

However I will tell you what happens. Nothing. The error goes undetected. Anyone who sends important data and cannot be bothered to do more than add a parity bit for safety deserves all that is coming to him.

Pascal

Blaise **Pascal** was a 17th-century mathematician who invented a mechanical calculating machine and thus got his handle on a programming language developed in Zürich in the 1970s.

Pascal is a high-level **language** which is popular in both scientific and technical programming. It is occasionally to be seen popping its head up in the world of commercial applications.

Patch

See **object code.**

PCM

PCM stands for both Plug Compatible Manufacturer and Plug Compatible Mainframe. See **plug compatible.**

PEEK

PEEK is a **BASIC** instruction which allows the **application program** to retrieve data from a specified byte number in memory (see **absolute addressing).**

This is usually done to read otherwise inaccessible information from the part of memory occupied by the systems software, for example to allow direct use of an **operating system** routine. Peeking is good fun so long as you can appreciate what you are looking at.

Peripherals

The central unit of a computer usually has a range of devices attached to it. The most common devices are printers and disk drives, but there is also a wide range of specialist devices of which **bar-code** readers and **MICR** readers are but two examples.

These devices are referred to as **peripherals,** peripheral units, or just PUs. Each is connected to the central unit by one or more of the forest of wires disappearing into the back of the main unit. If you are curious as to which wire connects which peripheral, the thing to do is to pull them out one at a time, watching to see which device fails. It is best to do this when there is nobody around.

Personal Computer

The advent of the microcomputer ushered in the low-cost computer. It became possible for people to afford their own computer, be it at home or in the office. These were variously called Home Computers, or Homebrews, **Personal Computers** (PCs), or Professional Computers (also PCs, naturally).

To me homebrew means odd-tasting brain-disorienting home-brewed bitter. If I were invited round to try someone's homebrew and were faced with a home computer I would be disappointed, to say the least.

The personal computer revolution has brought with it some extraordinary developments. Executives become obsessed with finding out how budget planning programs work, losing all track of day-to-day events. Sunday morning football fixture lists are run off on a computer in someone's spare bedroom. People in public bars ask you how a particular **BASIC** statement works. (The safe answer is 'slowly'.)

PERT

PERT stands for Project Evaluation and Review Technique.

This is a technique for planning out a **project** and monitoring its progress. It pays particular attention to tasks which are dependent on outside events, like the completion of other tasks, or the **hardware** for the development team arriving.

Any connection with 'pert' meaning 'perky' is purely coincidental. PERT planners there are. Perky planners there are not.

Picosecond

See **millisecond.**

PIN

PIN stands for Personal Identification Number. See **ATM.**

PL/1

PL/1 is a programming language modestly called Programming Language One.

It was designed to combine the capabilities of commercially oriented languages such as **COBOL** with those of scientifically oriented languages like **FORTRAN**.

This means that programmers can use a sub-set of a wide-ranging language rather than all of a small one.

'Big deal,' I hear you say, 'what is so good about that?'

If you find out, please let me know.

Plug Compatible

Once upon a time a customer who bought a **mainframe** from a manufacturer had no option but to buy all the associated **terminals** and **peripherals** from the same manufacturer.

This was good news for manufacturers who had sold mainframes and bad news for everybody else.

In due course other manufacturers started to penetrate this market by producing terminals and peripherals that could be used instead of those of the mainframe manufacturer. These replacements had to work completely compatibly so that the buyer could just plug them in. Hence **plug compatible** equipment and 'PCM' version one, being Plug Compatible Manufacturer.

What next? Replace the entire mainframe, of course. The customer can then get a cheaper mainframe without having to re-write any software. Enter 'PCM' version two, being Plug Compatible Mainframe.

POKE

POKE is a **BASIC** instruction which allows the programmer to 'POKE' a value into just about any memory location. The location is usually specified as an **absolute address.**

POKE is often used to change something in the part of memory occupied by the **systems software** to suit the convenience of a particular **application program.**

Of course you should not go poking the systems software around unless you know exactly where to poke it, and with what. In this respect the systems software is very like a donkey.

POS

POS stands for Point of Sale.

A POS **terminal** combines the functions of a cash register with those of a computer terminal or microcomputer.

You can often tell a POS terminal from an ordinary cash register by the bunch of cables emerging from the side of it and disappearing through a hole in the ceiling above. The cables usually look big enough to carry the power supply for a medium-sized city.

The POS terminal is able to transfer sales data to a central computer as the sales occur. This allows the central supplies department to react quickly to sales fluctuations, such as panic buying of oxtail soup or a Tuesday morning rush on plastic paint rollers.

Primary Key

See **key**.

Printers

Printers are **peripheral** devices which print out information as directed by a computer program.

There are several varieties of printer. The ever-popular **Dot-Matrix** and **Daisy-Wheel** are described in separate sections. Other types of printer include:

Barrel:
The barrel printer is so called because its main feature is a horizontal cylinder, or 'barrel'. The barrel comprises a set of rings, one for each print position. Each

ring has a complete character set on it and is located opposite its own 'hammer', with the paper and ink ribbon in between. As the entire barrel spins printing is achieved by the hammers smacking the ribbon and paper against the print rings as the required characters whizz past.

Thermal:
These printers form characters by burning the shape into special paper. They are also well suited to design printing as they can reproduce any shape.

Ink Jet:
These printers form characters by directing tiny ink jets at the paper.

So why bother printing on paper in an electronic world?

First, paper is considered more 'permanent', as reflected in the phrase 'hard copy', which is a print-out of a screen display or whatever. Second, technology has not yet threatened paper's greater convenience, in that it is not yet practical to check electronic information in the bath, at the bus stop, or while the children are talking at breakfast.

Processor

See **CPU.**

Program

A computer program defines a sequence of actions for the computer to carry out.

When the program is run it instructs the computer to carry out those actions. This is why the lines of a program are called instructions.

The actions may be purely internal, like adding one number to another, or external, like printing something or asking for a keyboard entry.

The only real problem with programs is the decision-making instructions. These decide what the program should do next, basing the decision on internal checks, or what key was pressed last, or any other variable condition.

It is the multitude of permutations and combinations of conditions that makes writing a program so very complicated.

A computer uses different types of programs. For more information see **application program, systems program** and **utility program.**

Remember that without a program the computer is about as intelligent as a steam iron, and a lot less use.

Program Development

The stages in **program development** are:

Define Requirements
This stage should not be missed. It is the job of the **systems analyst.** The analyst may provide detailed **specifications** for the programmer. There again, he may provide just a few sheets of paper. Or no sheets of paper, but a verbal briefing. In order to stop verbal briefings rambling on it is important to agree in advance when they will stop, for example when the analyst gets out at Oxford Circus.

Source Coding
The programmer writes the **source code** of the program, complaining about the specification all the way.

Compilation/Assembly
The program is converted from source code into **object code.** If the first attempt to do this is successful there is something weird going on.

Program Testing
The program is tested on its own, using test data. The actual data used may be the product of wild speculation by the programmer, or may be provided by the analyst.

Systems Testing
All the programs in a suite of programs are used together to see if they are compatible. Expertise in the art of Blame Avoidance is important for all involved.

After systems tests the program suite is ready to make its first nervous appearance in the real world. See **parallel run** and **implementation.**

Program Listing

A **program listing** is a computer print-out of the statements in a program. It is invaluable for error detection and correction.

It is advisable to be extremely conscientious about taking 'clean' program listings. Trying to locate a problem in a listing with changes scribbled all over it leaves the following areas of conjecture:

1. Were the intended changes ever actually introduced into the program?
2. If so, were they keyed in accurately?
3. Were they subsequently changed themselves?

4. Have all the program line numbers and addresses changed?
5. Why didn't the idle good-for-nothing take a clean listing?

If you are a weekend computer person who likes a drink or two at lunchtime the green pen technique may come in handy. All you have to do is use a blue pen for writing program changes on the listing before lunch, and use a green pen after lunch. This can save days by clearly indicating where to start looking for a bug that has suddenly got into the program.

Programmer

It is the programmer's job to write the **source code** for a program and get it working correctly.

The programmer finds out what a program should do by reading the **specification.** If the specification is too precise the programmer will complain that he is just being used as a coding machine. If it is not precise he will complain that he is being asked to do the impossible. Both reactions are entirely reasonable. I have been a programmer and I know.

Once a program has been compiled it has to be tested. It is at this stage that the programmer shows his real mettle. It takes a particular mentality to spend months carefully constructing something and then set about testing it to destruction.

Good programmers are able to do this. They show extraordinary perseverance, strength of mind and clarity of thought. They are also quick-witted, good-looking, charming, and generous to a fault. This is also true of many ex-programmers.

Program Specification

See **specifications.**

Program Testing

See **program development; programmer.**

Project

A **project** is something which will be done. Probably.

In the computer world the word 'project' implies a sizeable undertaking. This may be the development of an applications system or **operating system,** the creation of a new **network,** the production of new **hardware,** or getting the programmers to tidy up their listings.

Project Manager

Project managers are odd characters whose job it is to ensure that projects are successfully completed.

The people that a project manager should try to keep happy include the user department, the chief programmer, the **systems analysts,** the application programmers, the **technical programmers,** the trainers, the O & M department, the **operations department** and his own management.

In trying to keep these people happy the project manager will almost inevitably come into conflict with the user department, the chief programmer, the systems analysts, the application programmers, the technical programmers, the trainers, the O & M department, the operations department and his own management.

If you crave popularity, do not become a project manager.

Project managers, like **network** designers, must be paranoid optimists. Paranoia helps them predict and thus minimise the consequences of the myriad problems which will arise. Without paranoia they would never finish a project. Without optimism they would never get started.

PROM

PROM stands for Programmable Read Only Memory. It is used to describe this type of **chip.**

By definition, the areas of memory in **ROM** chips cannot be changed by a computer program. However, the contents, say the **BASIC interpreter** in a home computer, have to get into the chip sometime. This is achieved on a special machine which 'burns' the programs into a PROM, making it perfectly sensible for a production manager to ask for more burnt chips.

The main variations on the ROM theme are:

EAROM:.
Electrically Alterable ROM. Not strictly a ROM in that the contents can be changed electrically while the chip is in a computer. This 'reprogramming' is slow, however. EAROMs do not lose their contents when power is cut off, unlike most RAMs. EAROMs can be partially reprogrammed, unlike EPROMs.

EEROM:
Electrically Erasable ROM. EEROMs have the same characteristics as EPROMSs.

EPROM:
Erasable Programmable ROM. EPROMs can be cleared and reprogrammed, unlike PROMs which can only be programmed once. The clearing process gave rise to the unlikely sounding task of 'wiping an EPROM'. Programming is done on a special machine which uses ultraviolet light. Unlike EAROMs, EPROMs cannot be ***partially*** reprogrammed.

Some companies now supply home-computer **application programs** on PROMs. This means that instead of loading the program into RAM from disk or **cassette** you plug in the PROM. Try saying 'plug in a program PROM' quickly ten times in a row. You tried it? Idiot.

Protocol

A communications **protocol** defines a set of conventions to be used by computers or other intelligent devices when communicating with each other. The conventions cover the sequence and format of the messages to be exchanged, with the messages themselves comprising data and/or control information.

Take as an example the following sequence, which obeys the conventions of a simple protocol (also see **control characters**):

Computer A	Computer B	Comment
ENQ ——→		Is anybody there?
	←—— ACK	Yes, I heard you
Data1 ——→		Have some data
	←—— NAK	Sorry, didn't hear that clearly

Data1 ⟶ Here is the data again
⟵ ACK Got it
Data2 ⟶ Here is some more data
etc . . .

Without the protocol anything could happen:

Data1 ⟶ Have some data
⟵ NAK Sorry, didn't hear that clearly
Data2 ⟶ Have some more data
⟵ WAK Hang about! I'm not ready
Data3 ⟶ Have some more data
⟵ WAK Wait!
Data4 ⟶ Have some more data
etc . . .

There are hundreds of different protocols. They are usually designed for a particular type of communication as the requirements of an efficient protocol for, say, **batch communications** are very different from those for an **interactive** system.

This opens up areas of considerable challenge for the Computer Person, who frequently has to design a system using a completely inappropriate protocol. 'How come?', you ask. Sometimes the Computer Person gets pretty fed up with people asking stupid questions.

PSS

PSS stands for Packet Switch Stream. This is the name of the British Telecom packet switching **network.** See **packet switching** for an explanation of this type of communication system.

New computer developments tend to bring their own jargon with them. The PSS is no exception, ushering one into a world of CUGs, PADs and PVCs. For the curious these are:

PAD:

Packet Assembly/Disassembly Device, used for connections between the PSS and fairly stupid computers. Clever computers assemble and disassemble packets for themselves.

CUG:

Closed User Group, the member computers of which can only be called by other computers in the group. This provides some security against unauthorised access to private data.

PVC:
Permanent Virtual Circuit. A circuit joining two computers across the PSS which the computers see as being kept open permanently. The 'virtual' creeps in because the continuous switching of the route taken by messages means that although the 'logical' connection is permanent the physical circuit is not. For background see the entries on **packet switching** and **virtual.** If you are still not satisfied, get a bigger book.

PSTN

PSTN stands for Public Switched Telephone Network. This is the network that carries ordinary telephone calls.

PSTNs are invaluable to the computer industry because of their vast existing **networks.** Although they were designed for carrying voices they can also carry data through the use of boxes of electronic tricks such as **acoustic couplers** and **modems.**

A network of computers communicating over the PSTN has to have some way of dealing with the inevitable occasions when the switching goes up the swannee and a computer gets put through to a dentist's receptionist or a telephone under a bucket at a British Rail enquiry centre. See **protocol** for how this is handled.

Punched Cards

In the days before **magnetic-media** technology was commonly available, the **punched card** and **paper tape** were the main means of storing information, be it data or programs.

Cards were cheap and convenient. Information was stored by punching holes in selected positions in the card, which could subsequently be read into a computer. The cards were punched on special machines worked by 'key-punch operators', often in a non-alcoholic, non-pugilistic 'punch room'.

A collection of the tiny rectangles of card that are removed to leave the holes is called chad. In the good old days pieces of chad were poked back into holes which had been punched in the wrong place. Nowadays the life cycle of the typical card is:

1. Be manufactured
2. Have some holes punched in it
3. Be read into a computer
4. Be thrown away

This is called limited re-usability, poor cyclability, inflexibility modification-wise, or doing the only sensible thing with a card with a load of holes in it.

PUT

The **PUT** statement is common to many languages. It instructs the **processor** to put a record from memory to a **file,** the file being on a storage medium such as a disk or tape.

PUT is a frequent rather than ever-present player in teams of **BASIC** instructions. The first three BASIC manuals checked gave these different instructions for transferring data to files:

1. PUT used for **random access** files
   WRITE Used for **sequential access** files
2. PUT Used for all files
   WRITE Not used at all
3. PUT Not used at all
   WRITE Not used at all

So what instruction do you use in version 3? 'PRINT', of course. Good old BASIC.

PVC

PVC stands for Permanent Virtual Circuit. See **PSS.** If you think you can make jackets out of it, you are not yet a Computer Person.

RAM

This stands for 'Random Access Memory', which means that you can go poking it about.

The essential thing about **RAM,** as opposed to **ROM,** is that it can be and is changed while the computer is running. RAM therefore holds the programs loaded in, from disk for example, plus all the associated data which those programs are processing. RAM can hold one program at one time and a different one at a different time.

RAM size is therefore very important in determining how big a program a computer is capable of running.

Random Access

Be warned. When a Computer Person uses the word 'random' he probably does not mean random at all. If a program is accessing anything randomly the program is what is technically known as 'buggered'.

Random access usually means that you can get at any part of something directly, that is to say without looking through from the beginning. This could

be a disk file, or memory (see **RAM**).

It can be compared to finding, say, the 'Tomorrow and tomorrow and tomorrow Creeps in this petty pace from day to day To . . .' in a copy of ***Macbeth.*** If you do not know where it is you would probably look through from the start, i.e. sequentially. But if you are some kind of Smart Alec and know which page it is on you can go straight there.

This, believe it or not, is what the Computer Person calls random access.

READ

READ is an instruction in many languages. It tells the **processor** to transfer a record from a **storage** medium such as a disk into the computer memory.

READ also exists in some versions of **BASIC** in combination with the 'DATA' statement. Here the READ assigns the names of **variables** to data **fields,** the value of which is specified in a DATA statement.

For example, take a pools checking program which has to set up the number of points for each type of result, for use later in the program:

```
10      DATA 3,2,1.5,1
        ......
100     READ SCOREDRAW, NOSCOREDRAW, AWAYWIN, HOMEWIN
        ......
```

This has exactly the same effect as:

```
100     LET SCOREDRAW=3
101     LET NOSCOREDRAW=2
102     LET AWAYWIN=1.5
103     LET HOMEWIN=1
```

Including the field values within the program itself like this is called 'hard coding' the data. This is complete anathema to the Computer Person. Data should be in **files.** It should never, ever, ever, be necessary to re-compile a program just to change data.

However, when computers start to appear in the spare bedroom something has to suffer, be it professional norms, or just the visiting aunt who now has to sleep in the bath.

Real-Time Communications

A **real-time communications** system is one in which the data entered on remote **terminals** immediately updates records on a central computer.

Fortune favours the bold.

Real-time updating is an essential feature of some systems. The usual example is the airline-ticket booking system, in which the central records must reflect the number of tickets sold for a particular flight, minute by minute.

Record

A **record** is a group of associated data **fields** which are recorded on a **storage** device.

For example, a payroll system would have a record for each member of staff. Each record contains fields such as hourly rate of pay, tax code and so forth. The full set of records form the payroll **file**, which may co-exist with other files on a disk, or 'volume'.

That is to say that a field is in a record is in a file is in a volume.

Recovery

See **fallback**.

Redundancy Check

The **redundancy check** is a system for detecting corruption within a block of data.

This is very important. One bit in your payroll **record** being set to the wrong value because of a flaw on a disk or interference on a communications line (called a 'glitch') could halve your rate of pay, double your tax bill or change your sex.

The redundancy check works by the originating computer adding extra 'check' characters to a block of data before sending it to an outside device. The value of the check characters is determined by a computation involving all the characters in the main block. The receiving computer performs the same computation on the main block and compares its own result to the check characters sent with the block. If the two are not the same something has been corrupted en route and the block is rejected; if they are the same then the block is accepted, with the now redundant check characters being thrown away.

There is always the possibility that compensatory errors will lead to the check characters being right by chance. However it is not prohibitively expensive to use redundancy check systems which reduce the possibility of undetected errors to practically zero.

This is a shame. Sorting out the consequences of errors which have slipped through is one of the most stimulating things that can happen to a Computer Person. Indeed, he will often get so involved that he will work all night, gently encouraged by management remarks like 'no one goes anywhere until it's sorted out'.

REM

The **BASIC** statement **REM,** for 'Remark', allows the programmer to add comments to the **program listing.** A REM in no way affects the way in which the program runs.

Remarks are designed to help somebody who has to change the program to understand what it is doing. For example:

```
10 LET DZ%=Z%(ZB%*(ZA%/2)+1)-10*(ZB%+ZA%(ZA%/ZB%+2))
20 REM DON'T CHANGE LINE 10! IT WORKS, BUT NOBODY KNOWS
       WHY.
```

Resource

Computer Persons use **resource** to get a computer system up and running. Resource is mostly personnel.

Personnel used to be referred to as resources but the final 's' is on the way out. I have known programmers get pretty upset on being told officially that they are no longer a resource. I can understand their point of view. Being called a resource is bad enough, but it is a lot better than being called ***some*** resource.

Restart

When an operator turns a computer off, having completed a program run, the subsequent commencement of work is simply called a 'start'.

When the cleaner turns the computer off by pulling its plug out of the

socket in the middle of a program run in order to plug in a vacuum cleaner the subsequent commencement of work is called a **'restart'.**

Systems designers aim to ensure that restarts can be handled easily, with no loss of data and without having to start the run from the beginning again. This is usually achieved by writing vital information, such as totals accumulated during the run, onto a disk at selected points in the program. The idea is that the program can restart from that point (the 'checkpoint') if necessary by reading the 'secured' information from the disk.

RETURN

See **GOSUB/RETURN.**

ROM

This stands for Read Only Memory. The computer cannot change its contents, which means that it is no use at all for data or your own programs.

The **ROM** contains the basic intelligence of the machine, such as the thing which displays a message saying 'put a disk in, dummy' and then loads the system when the disk has been put in (see **bootstrap**). It is therefore permanently resident (or 'hard-wired') in the ROM **chip** (see **PROM**).

ROM can also contain **systems programs.** This avoids loading them into the machine each time it is turned on. (See **when hard, when soft?**)

Apart from first loading the machine, you will probably only hear from the ROM if something goes wrong: for example, a message on the screen saying 'ROM ERROR'.

If this happens do not bother looking for loose connections in the chip. Turn the computer off and turn it on again. This may fix the problem. If it does work be happy and do not worry about it.

RS-232

RS-232C is the EIA (Electronic Industries Association of Great Britain) standard for the **serial interface** between a computer **terminal** and communications devices such as **modems.** It is broadly equivalent to **CCITT** Recommendation Number V24.

In practice these standards are most commonly used for the interface between computers and **peripherals,** where there is a similar requirement for the controlled transfer of data. The standards define the use of each of the twenty-five connecting wires.

Most connections use only a few of these, making it possible to answer the question 'What on earth are all these wires for?' in just an hour or two. The answer to the similar question 'Which of all these wires is for the earth?' is 'Number seven', incidentally.

Run Time

Run time is the time during which a computer is used for its designated purpose.

It can be important to know how long a program will take to run, particularly if you want to arrange to meet someone in a pub afterwards, or if you are responsible for deciding how powerful a computer to buy.

There are two ways of timing a program. One is to measure the 'elapsed time', being the time which passes from start point to finish point. However, as all sizeable machines run several programs at once (see **multiprogramming**), the elapsed time for a particular program will vary according to how many other programs are sharing the **processor**'s time. The second timing criterion is therefore 'processor' time, being the total time that the processor is actually required.

It is clear from this that it is not always possible to be precise about when a program run will finish. This is why it is better for operators to arrange to meet people in saloon bars, rather than outdoors where it might be raining.

Scheduling

Scheduling is the job of arranging the tasks that must be completed to finish a **project,** into a plan.

The computer industry's history of scheduling errors makes house builders seem to have divine foresight. The difficulty arises through the extreme complexity of a computer system, and the computer's intolerance of any deviation from perfection.

However nobody will thank the scheduler if he is right, and everyone will blame him if he is wrong. This is why it is foolish to help a scheduler; only harm can come of it. Being a scheduler is tedious, joyless, thankless, dangerous, miserable and thoroughly depressing.

It is surprising that schedulers are not more bad tempered than they are. If you meet a scheduler, you should buy him a drink.

The scheduling principle NOT to follow is 'schedule completion for the first date for which you cannot prove that completion is absolutely impossible'.

Screen

The **screen** is attached to a computer or computer **terminal** so that the operator can see what is going on. If he looks, of course.

'Screen' is a bit short but it can be lengthened to 'monitor'. This can then be lengthened to 'Visual Display Unit', which in its turn can be shortened to 'VDU'.

Screen Formatter

A **screen formatter** is a **software tool** which makes it easy for the **application program** to set up **fields** on a screen and handle new fields as they are entered through the keyboard.

A formatter usually consists of a routine which is used by the main program whenever it has any dealings with the screen or keyboard. The routine does all the tricky bits, like sending special characters to the screen to identify the row and column position for the **cursor,** or checking that the operator has not keyed an alpha character into a numeric field.

Screen formatters are satisfying to write because the results of one's labours can be seen so immediately. Give a Computer Person a micro and he will immediately write a screen formatter for it, whether or not it already has one. Talk to a traditional Computer Person about the best software he ever wrote and he will invariably tell you about his screen formatter.

This is clearly ridiculous. Curiously, but quite by chance, the best thing that I ever wrote myself was in fact a screen formatter. Mine was special, though. All the application program had to do . . .

Secondary Key

See **key**.

Sector

See **disks–general.**

Semi-Byte

A **semi-byte** is half a byte, or four bits.

It can hold 16 different values, 0000 (decimal or **hexadecimal** '0') to 1111 (decimal '15' or hexadecimal 'F').

A semi-byte is handy because it is the smallest number of bits necessary to hold the 10 different values of a decimal digit (3 bits can only hold 8 values). You therefore need a semi-byte to hold a decimal digit, whether in computer memory or on a **floppy disk.**

You may on occasion come across specialist computer fraternities who also talk about 'nibbles'. There is always somebody who does not know when he is taking a good thing too far.

Sequential Access

Sequential access describes the accessing of a series of items in the sequence in which they are held.

This is fine for some situations and not for others.

For example consider a **file** of debit transactions which have to be allocated to the appropriate bank account **records.** Reading the transaction records themselves sequentially is perfectly satisfactory. However, having read a transaction, the system needs to find the record of the account which the transaction affects. It would clearly be crazy to search through the account file one record at a time until the correct record was found. In this instance **random access** is required in preference to sequential access.

Of course if your file is on a **cassette** and there are 15 metres of magnetic tape between its current position and the required record, the fanciest random access method in the world will not be much help to you.

In real life this would not happen. Banks can afford **disks.**

Serial Interface

In a **serial interface** the data bits move down a single **channel** one after the other, like railway trains. This is different from the **parallel interface** in which groups of bits arrive together, like London buses.

Software

A computer is delivered to a User's premises in boxes. The boxes contain the computer **hardware,** being keyboards, screens, sets of circuit boards, disk drives, enough different cables to threaten the mere existence of the word 'standardisation' and whatever else is part of the **configuration.**

This lot is connected together by a genius masquerading as an engineer, or as your ten-year-old son. It can then be plugged in and turned on, a few lights may come on, with a message or two on the screen, and then . . . nothing.

The computer is now waiting for some **software.** If you do not have any you should either go and get some or forget the whole stupid idea.

The software will be loaded into the computer from some outside medium. This will normally be from a **floppy disk,** a **hard disk,** a **cassette,** or a deck of **punched cards.** You may even key the program in each time, if you're a masochist.

The software is anything loaded in by these means. It is called soft because it is not permanently resident in the computer, in that it is not 'burnt' or 'hard-wired' into a **chip.** It is read into the **RAM** each time it is needed.

It is also called soft because it is relatively easy to change. You can compare software and hardware to plasticine and concrete if you think it will do you any good. Only do not take the comparison too far. Software is not tangible like plasticine, in that you cannot get it under your fingernails.

For more information on the different kinds of software see **application**

program, systems program, utility program and **operating system.** Some old-timers still use 'software' to mean just the systems software. This is obviously ridiculous. Software is any sort of program which has to be read into the computer.

Software Factory

This is an unappealing description of a location where a team of people is working on **software** production.

It is not unknown for a Computer Person to be employed in a **software factory** as a software foreman, only to find that there are no software workers. This is not a good situation to get into.

Software House

Software house is the industry name for a company specialising in **software** writing. This could be **application programs** or specialist **systems programs.**

Software houses can be any size, and there are a great many one-man bands in addition to the larger and more substantial organisations. One software house I know plays prop forward, weighs seventeen stone and can drink up to fifteen pints of heavy in a session. He therefore comes into both categories.

Software Tool

A **software tool** is something that helps with the production of a program.

An example is a standard piece of **software** for doing a particular job, which the programmer uses in different programs rather than re-writing it each time.

Another type of tool is one which makes writing part of the program easier than if it were done using the normal programming language. A common example of this is a **screen formatter,** which allows a programmer to describe a screen layout quickly and easily.

Some software tools even provide easy ways to create entire programs. These are called program generators.

Use of the term 'software tool' to describe a programmer is impolite.

Sort

Some processes need the **records** in a **file** to be in order. The order is determined by the contents of the **key field** within each record, the records usually being arranged so that the keys are in ascending order.

Take as an example a file of payroll records. The key field is the personnel number. The records must be arranged so that these numbers are in ascending order to allow the payslips to be printed in the right sequence.

Any necessary arranging is done by a **utility program** called a **sort,** sometimes in combination with a 'merge' program which merges together two or more sorted files.

Efficient sorts are very difficult to write, and literally hundreds of different techniques have been used. A technique is normally best suited to a particular situation. A sort which was designed for a file which starts in completely haphazard order will not be the best to use for a file with just a few records out of place. Unless the sort was badly designed of course, which is quite possible.

The naming of sort techniques is an art in itself. The most popular include the ripple sort, the polyphase sort, the bubble sort, the cascade sort, the classical sort, the tree sort and the wonderful-sounding oscillating sort.

Source Code

Programs start life as a series of statements, written in a language and usually recorded on a **storage** medium such as a disk. This series of statements is where it all begins and is thus called **source code.**

The source code has to be converted into **object code** before it can be used, or 'run'. This is done by a **compiler** or **assembler.**

The simplest way to change a program is to change the source code and then re-create new object code through further use of the compiler or assembler. This makes the source code very valuable, which is why Computer Person will rarely hand over the source.

Object code can be modified to some extent by a programmer changing the bit patterns directly; this is called 'patching' or 'zapping' the code.

It is clearly foolhardy to start zapping the object code if you do not understand it fully. However, the format of the code will not be explained in any generally released manual, so if you like excitement you will just get on with it. This is also the best way to learn, and the greater the size of the consequent disaster the quicker the learning process. This is just as well because the greater the size of the disaster the less the time that you have left before you get sacked.

Specifications

Specifications are so called because they specify what a computer system should do. They are usually written by **systems analysts.**

The abbreviation for specification is 'spec', pronounced 'speck' rather than the more accurate 'spess' used in the building trade.

Different people expect different things to be in different types of specification, making it possible to give only a very general description of each one:

Functional Specification:
This defines the functions that a system will provide, that is what it will do rather than how it will do it.

Technical Specification:
This defines the technical detail of how a system works, for example by specifying the data that is passed between different programs.

Operational Specification:
This defines the system from the operator's viewpoint, for example by detailing screen layouts and keyboard use. It is often incorporated within one of the other specifications.

Program Specification:
This defines what a program should do in detail. Program specs can be pretty hard for the casual reader to understand. Unfortunately they can also be pretty hard for programmers to understand.

System Specification:
This can include any combination or permutation of the above, plus all sorts of other things.

Some people argue that specifications are easiest to write after the programs have been written. This is true. Unfortunately the programs are correspondingly easier to write after the specifications have been finished.

Spreadsheet

A **spreadsheet** is a program which allows the user to set up a series of relationships between different **fields** so that the entry of values into 'source' fields automatically changes the value of dependent fields.

Take as an extremely simple example a football league table where the source fields are the number of games played, the number won, the number drawn, the number of goals for and the number of goals against. A spreadsheet program can work out from these the number of games lost, the goal difference and the total points awarded.

The information is set out as a matrix, say with each row being for one team and each column being for one of the field types. Each field in the matrix is called a 'cell' and is either entered or contains a formula by which it can be calculated from other fields, say 'goal difference' equals 'goals for' minus 'goals against' for each team.

The full matrix can be pretty big. The user can look at a small section of this 'spread' sheet at any one time through the **window** of the computer screen. The whole spreadsheet can be seen by moving the window around, with the operator trying not to get too dizzy.

Spreadsheets can also be used for cricket averages and five-year-plans for multinational corporations.

Statement

A program is written as a series of **statements.**

The words used in statements must conform to the rules of a programming **language.** The statements include executive instructions which tell the computer **processor** what to do and declarative instructions which do things like reserve areas of memory for the **storage** of data.

State of The Art

'State of the art' is a phrase used as both an adjective and a noun. There are two types of reaction to its use, typified by:

1. 'He kept saying "state of the art." I was really impressed.'
2. 'He kept saying "state of the art." Only a complete idiot would be impressed by that.'

State-of-the-art technology is that which incorporates the very latest developments, otherwise known as those at the 'leading edge' of technology. If you find yourself in front of the leading edge of technology you had better watch out.

STOP

STOP is a program instruction which is common to a number of high-level **languages,** including **COBOL, FORTRAN** and **BASIC.** It stops the program and tells the computer to get ready to run another (or to re-run the same one).

If you have got to the point of only being able to think in BASIC it may help to see this exotic instruction in its natural habitat:

```
5000 STOP
```

Storage

Storage is a hopelessly vague term for describing anything or anywhere that stores data and/or programs.

Storage can be computer memory, either **RAM** or **ROM,** and 'backing storage' devices such as disk drives or **magnetic tapes.** I do not suppose anybody would object if you also used it to describe the room where the computer paper is stored.

It is clearly important to be careful in the use of 'storage'. Nobody who thinks he has asked his manager for more RAM in the computer wants to end up with use of a cupboard in the back of the stationery room.

String

There are two types of **string** in the computer world. Neither of them come in balls. With so much wire around who needs balls of string?

The first string is a stream of data items organised sequentially according to the value of some sort of key.

The second string is breeding uncontrollably in the world of micro-computers. It is a **field** of consecutive characters, often called a string **variable.** This sort of field can hold alphabetic as well as numeric characters, and is thus different from a numeric variable.

Structured Programming

The highly technological computer industry traditionally has had an extra-ordinarily casual approach to the matter of how programs should be written.

This casualness is particularly odd given that a high proportion of the cost of producing a system lies in programming time.

Enter Professor Dijkstra and the concept of **structured programming.** This imposes a discipline on programming style, which is no bad thing for a lot of programmers.

The most famous structuring technique is that developed by a Michael Jackson who was not a pop musician. His technique is based on the linking of the program structure to that of the data that the program is manipulating. Reasonable structure can also be achieved through adhering to rules which define methods for the handling of repeated processes, sequences of processes and **subroutines.**

The techniques avoid the unpredictable leaps from one part of a program to another which make the subsequent introduction of modifications so hazardous. Therefore anybody sensible will ensure a disciplined structure in his programs.

Some modern languages are actually designed to impose a structure on the programmer. The traditional programmer has to draw on all his experience to work round this.

Subroutine

A **subroutine** is a section of program which is used often.

It can be called on as required by whichever part of the main program needs it, and there is no need to repeat the instructions of the subroutine all over the place. See **GOSUB/RETURN** for an illustration of this.

Subroutines can themselves call other subroutines, creating a 'nesting' effect of subroutines being called from within others. Done properly this is an aid to a reasonable structure in a program.

If it is done imaginatively, with a few **GOTO**-like hyperspace journeys, it helps the Data Processing Manager on the way to his next nervous breakdown. This sort of thing is done by Real Programmers to keep up their interest in the job. It can save a few bytes of memory, or trim a nanosecond or two off a program's execution time. It also makes the program impossible to change because nobody, including the original programmer, can understand how it works.

Symbolic Addressing

A program must have a means of specifying which data **field** it wants to access or which program instruction it wishes to branch to. Both are held at addresses in the computer's memory.

In order to save the programmer having to mess around with actual byte numbers (see **absolute addressing**) the **compilers, interpreters** and **assemblers** let him use symbolic names in his **source code**, converting them to physical memory addresses for him.

Selecting the symbolic names is one of the few chances that a programmer gets to show some literary imagination. This results in instructions like OPEN SESAME, GOTO PIECES, CALL BOX, COMMON LAND and CHAIN SMOKER.

I used to do this sort of thing a lot. It seemed quite funny at the time.

Synchronous Communication

In the bad old days before books like this were about it took me ages to get a grip on the difference between **asynchronous** and **synchronous communication.**

In fact it is very simple. In asynchronous systems each character travels from one device to the other on its own, like drips from a tap. Each one needs its own 'start' and 'stop' bits.

In a synchronous system characters are grouped together and sent in synchronised 'blocks', each block having some header and trailer characters.

Synchronous systems are much more efficient when it comes to transferring a lot of characters quickly and securely. It is not so easy to ensure the safe arrival of the lone travellers of an asynchronous **network.**

Systems Analyst

In order to write a useful **application program** the programmer must be told exactly what the program should do.

The alternative is to leave all the details to the programmer's imagination. This would be similar to asking a bricklayer to build a cathedral, designing it as he goes.

The person most likely to know what the programs should do is the user. However the user knows nothing about the computer. He is therefore unable to judge the feasibility of what he wants, the implications of alternative approaches, or any requirements for **compatibility** with existing programs.

So why not leave the user to discuss the matter with the programmer?

Are you crazy?

Would you get the bishop to discuss the cathedral with the bricklayer, then let the bricklayer get on with it?

Enter the **systems analyst,** or simply 'analyst'.

It is his job to work out what the programs should do, co-operating with the user, and checking programming complications with the specialist programmers as necessary. He writes the results of this down in a **specification.**

Some analysts start with experience as a user but know little about the computer. Others start with experience of the computer, but know little or nothing about the user department. Another group is blissfully unhampered by any preconceptions in that they know nothing about either. Somebody once told me that he knew somebody whose sister had once been engaged to an analyst who knew about both, but most of them have to work out what on earth is going on as the **project** proceeds.

When the time comes to allocate the blame for Whatever Went Wrong the analyst fits the bill nicely, being largely unable to defend himself. This seems to me to be entirely reasonable, not being an analyst.

The systems analyst, then, liaises between the user and the programmer, with the aim of producing a specification for a set of application programs which keeps the user not too unhappy and does not prompt the programmer to down tools. He does all this knowing that his objective is virtually unattainable.

The question 'Why would anybody intelligent want to be an analyst?' is a tricky one for a non-analyst to deal with.

Systems Program

An **application program** can cause complex sequences of events to occur by single instructions. A simple **WRITE** instruction on an intelligent **terminal** could well result in a record being recorded on a disk on a **mainframe** system several hundred miles away.

The sequence of events is handled by the computer's **operating system,** which is itself a set of specialist programs called **systems programs,** or systems software.

The systems programs are written and poked around by people called systems programmers, or **technical programmers.**

Systems programmers are distinguished by an ability to do mental arithmetic in **binary**.

Systems Software

See **systems program**.

Systems Specification

See **specifications**.

Systems Testing

See **program development**.

Tape Streamer

Hard disks are becoming smaller and cheaper. Microcomputer users can now enjoy the advantages of a hard disk's **storage** capacity and access speeds, both of which are a considerable improvement over the **floppy disk**.

This introduces the problem of how to take a back-up copy of the contents of the hard disk, for use should the disk fail. Feeding 30 floppies into a microcomputer one after the other gradually to copy off the contents of a hard disk is uncomfortably like cooking the toast for breakfast at a large hotel using only one toaster.

The solution is the **tape streamer** which is used for a copy, or 'dump', of the complete contents of the hard disk onto a cartridge-like tape. This can be used to restore the contents in their entirety if required. A tape streamer is small, quick and cheap, and is only fully appreciated by those who have served time as assistant cooks at hotels.

TDM

TDM stands for Time Division Multiplexing. See **multiplexing.**

Technical Programmer

The **technical,** or 'systems', **programmer** is a bit-freak whose job it is to write and maintain the systems software.

He lives in a mysterious world of intricate programs written in low-level **languages.** Because of the complexity of most systems software, technical programmers tend to specialise. This makes it difficult for them to help each other much, which explains why they spend so much time staring at unfathomable displays on their **terminals** or buried in incomprehensible manuals.

The Ballad of the Technical Programmer

It looks as though his future,
Lies in front of a computer,
With a manual for a tutor
He should really have some fun.

He'll write his code quite clearly,
With accuracy, or nearly,
And if errors cost him dearly
He'll not blame his mother's son.

And close to tears though he may verge
Because he's problems with a merge
He'll manfully resist the urge
To pack his bags and run.

He'll treat with due enormity
Each system non-conformity;
He'll attack each new deformity
Till opening time has come.

He'll be bugger and debugger
He'll be source-code-error mugger
He'll be disk and manual lugger
Till his software days are done.

Technical Specification

See **specifications.**

Teletype

The **Teletype** Corporation of America has lent its name as an extremely general descriptor of a range of devices.

'Teletype' devices are those which combine some of the characteristics of a typewriter with an ability to use telecommunications systems. They can be used for keying in and transmitting outgoing messages or for receiving and printing incoming messages. Teletype, or TTY, is also used to describe the simple **asynchronous communication** techniques employed.

The most famous teletype machine in Britain was that used to print out the football results on the BBC's ***Grandstand*** on Saturday afternoons. It was called the teleprinter (not the telly printer), but sadly is in use no longer. It had to run out of paper eventually.

Terabyte

A **terabyte** is a TERrifically Astronomical number of bytes:
1 **Kilobyte** (K) = 1024 bytes (approx 1 thousand)
1 **Megabyte** (M) = 1024^2 bytes (approx 1 million)
1 **Gigabyte** (G) = 1024^3 bytes (approx 1 American billion)
1 **Terabyte** (T) = 1024^4 bytes (approx 1 British billion)

Terminal

A **terminal** is a workstation connected to a central computer. It usually comprises a minimum of a screen and keyboard, and may include other devices such as a printer, disk drive or complete cash register (see **POS**).

There are two main types of terminal.

'Dumb' terminals are those which are not themselves programmable, and are controlled by programs on the computer to which they are connected. They are also called 'NITS', for Non-Intelligent Terminals. A friend of mine at school was also called NIT. John, where are you now?

Intelligent terminals are programmable and 'talk' to the central computer under the control of their own local program. Unlike dumb terminals they can work as independent microcomputers should the central computer not be available.

It is perfectly all right not to discriminate between dumb and intelligent terminals when it comes to muttering, hissing or shouting 'You stupid computer!'

Thermal Printer

See **printers**.

Track

See **disks–general**.

TTY

See **Teletype.**

Turnkey System

Many organisations buy computers and then do their own **program development.** Sometimes, however, a computer company is asked to supply a complete working system.

This is called a **turnkey system,** on the basis that all the customer has to do is turn the key to 'ON' and start using the system. All the supplier has to do is make sure that it works perfectly.

Over-run against schedule on a turnkey system brings with it late delivery to the customer and an increase in cost to the supplier. This is why turnkey system production is no place for the faint-hearted.

One benefit enjoyed by staff working in this field is that they rarely get bored, except during the convalescent periods after heart attacks.

UNIX

The **UNIX operating system** was originally developed in A T & T's Bell Laboratories by two people who were dissatisfied with the speed of the operating system that they had to use for **program development.** UNIX is based on some elements of that original system.

The current version is written in the **'C'** language, which was developed by the same team.

The fact that UNIX is written in a high-level **language** makes it relatively easy to run on different computer **processors.** The main need is for a C language

compiler to convert the UNIX **source code** to the **machine code** of a particular processor. Most operating systems are written in the **assembly language** of a particular processor and thus need to be re-written to be usable elsewhere.

The original UNIX designed for program development use is now the basis for a proliferation of versions for commercial systems. Do not get carried away and start knocking up a new operating system of your own. Nobody knows how many people have become frustrated by a slow development environment, set out to write their own operating system, and are still at it.

Unpacked Data

See **packed data.**

User

The only black cloud in the Computer Person's otherwise clear blue sky is that somebody may actually want to use a finished system for doing something useful.

This black cloud is called the **user.**

Some users not only want to use a system, they want to start using it from the moment it is supposed to be ready. This is all very distressing for certain breeds of Computer Person. These breeds dream of a world free of users and, presumably, free of anyone footing the bill.

User Friendly

A **user friendly** system is one which uses day-to-day language to give the user lots and lots of easy-to-understand directions and prompts.

Producing this sort of system is extremely disturbing emotionally for the traditional Computer Person.

The difference between a traditional screen message and a user friendly

message is best illustrated by an example, where the operator is being warned that the printer has run out of paper:

Traditional: 'WRN*Z4/PR/B205*414*HR88'
User friendly: 'THE PRINTER'S RUN OUT OF PAPER AGAIN, YOU PRAT'

Utility Program

In order to develop an **application program** for a computer, and subsequently run it in a system, you need to be able to do various things.

To start with you need something which will let you key your own program into a machine, and modify it once it is there. You also need something to convert it to usable form, something to take a copy of the disk you have saved it on as a safeguard, and something to move it around from one disk to another. You will also need something to tell you what you already have on a disk, or to print out the contents of a data **file,** or erase a file, or create a new file, or take a copy of the disk with all the data files on as a safeguard.

In short you need a bit of help.

The 'somethings' which provide this help are appropriately called **utility programs,** or utilities. They are an essential part of any **operating system** because of the services that they perform, both for the programmer and the user.

Utilities are very powerful, for example in letting you copy one disk completely over another. When using utilities you should therefore bear in mind this cautionary rhyme:

The ability to copy,
From an all-important floppy,
To a disk which once held rubbish
Keeps your system safe and sound.
Either sooner though, or later,
You may lose your vital data,
Over-written by the rubbish
With the disks the wrong way round.

So read instructions warily,
Don't take risks voluntarily,
The consequence of errors
Must be thought of with alarm.
Approach with due humility
Each heaven-sent utility
Whose power to do you good
Is also power to do you harm.

V24

See **RS-232.**

Variable

A **variable** is a **field** in a program the value of which can be varied by the program.

In 'LET RATE=25' 'RATE' is the variable and '25' is called a constant. A constant is a field which is not changed, except by mistake or by an old-time programmer being clever.

VDU

See **screen.**

Verification

See **data validation.**

Virtual

The Computer Person uses the adjective '**virtual**' to describe something which he is pretending exists, even though he knows that in fact it does not exist at all.

It is doing this sort of thing that gives the Computer Person a bad name.

An example is virtual memory, the use of which allows a **mainframe** computer simultaneously to run a great many more programs than its physical memory has room for.

It is able to do this because it can process program instructions extremely quickly, 20 million per second (or 20 **MIPS**) not being unusual. If a **data-entry** program uses 100 instructions to process each of 5 characters per second keyed in by an operator it is obviously not even scratching the surface of the processor's power.

In order to use this spare capacity the computer will dump whole memory areas, program, data and all, onto disks for the 'spare' sections of time. It can then call in another program, run that for a while, dump that, call in another, and so on. The sections of time involved are tiny fractions of a second.

The net result of this is that the computer ***appears*** simultaneously to be running far more programs than its physical memory can hold. That is, it has virtual extra memory, also known as virtual **storage** (VS).

VLSI

See **LSI**.

When Hard, When Soft?

The **systems programs** are all the complicated programs which let you run your own **application programs.**

On some computers the systems programs are always loaded in from disk. Once they have been loaded in they stay resident in a **RAM chip** until either they are replaced with different systems programs, or the computer is turned off. This is clearly a very flexible arrangement.

However, if the computer is always going to use the same systems programs there is precious little point in messing about loading them into the RAM every time you turn on. In this case it makes a lot more sense to burn the program into a **ROM** chip in the first place. Once the system is running it does not make a lot of odds if the program started off in a chip or had to be loaded in there from a disk.

A good example is the complicated program which makes it possible to run an application program written in **BASIC.** This program is called an **interpreter.** The interpreter is resident in ROM in a home computer which only ever runs BASIC programs. However it would be read in to RAM from disk on a bigger computer which is also used to run different types of program which do not need the interpreter.

All this means is that in situations where there is no advantage in holding a program as software it can be burnt into the hardware once and for all. Once there, it is still a program, but it is no longer software.

WHILE/WEND

The most poetic pair of statements in **BASIC**, though many versions of the language do not include them.

Ah me! While wending through the woods one day, I saw the elves and pixies play, I stopped to . . .

Anyway, **WHILE/WEND** works something like this:

```
10    Open a bottle of wine
20    WHILE there is still wine in the bottle
30    Pour another glass of wine and drink it
40    WEND
50    GOTO 10
```

Statement 40 has the effect of returning the program to step 20, so long as the 'WHILE' condition is true. Once it ceases to be true the program will carry on to step 50.

Winchester Disk

See **hard disk**.

Window

Many computer systems have more information available for display than can be accommodated physically on the screen.

There are two common examples of this. The first is the **spreadsheet** program where the complete spreadsheet is many times the screen size. The second is a **multiprogramming** system on a microcomputer where two or more programs can be running at the same time, even if there is only one screen and keyboard.

In both cases the screen becomes a **window** in that it allows the operator to see only a part of the complete display. Some systems even allow the screen to be split into a number of small windows. I cannot handle this sort of thing myself. Anyone who has tried to watch Lee Trevino pitching up to the green on the left-hand side of a television screen at the same time as watching Tom Watson going for a birdie putt on the right will know what I mean.

Word Processor

A **word processor** is a computer which is programmed to help in the production of documents.

It does this by providing facilities for the entry, storage, modification and reproduction of text. In other words you can key things in, save them, get them back, poke them about and eventually print them out. This is particularly beneficial in the repetitive production of a standard letter, or in the production of tidy and accurate documents such as reports.

The first generation of word processors were designed for word processing ('WP') alone. However modern microcomputers are versatile enough to be used for both normal data processing and for the text manipulation requirements of word processing. The word processor is then simply another program, and the computer's versatility is known as 'multi-functionality', or being able to do all kinds of stuff.

WRITE

WRITE is an instruction in many programming languages. It instructs the computer to write a **record** from memory to a **peripheral** such as a disk or **magnetic tape.**

In some languages, including **COBOL,** the WRITE instruction is also used for **output** to a printer. As a contrast, and as noted elsewhere, at least one version of **BASIC** includes neither **PUT** nor WRITE and therefore has to use the PRINT instruction for output to a disk or tape. Hmmm.

X25

See **packet switching.**

You are now at the end of the main set of definitions.
Congratulations.

SUPPLEMENT 1

Binary Arithmetic

As mentioned in the main text, this is a very famous and little understood form of arithmetic.

It is different from decimal arithmetic in that it uses something called 'bits' rather than the decimal digits 0 to 9.

A bit is like an on/off switch. It can have two different values, 1 if on, or 0 if off.

If one bit can have two different values, 1 or 0, then two in combination can have four:

One Bit:	0	off
	or 1	on
Two Bits:	00	
	01	
	10	
	11	

This is very like combining digits for decimal numbers, but using bits (each having two possible values) rather than digits (each having ten possible values, 0 to 9):

Two Bits   00 01 10 11
(4 possible values, 00 to 11 inclusive)

Two Digits   00 01 02 03 04 05 06 07 08 09
10 11 12 13 14 ......
20 21 22 23 24 ...... etc up to 99
(100 possible values, 00 to 99 inclusive)

If you want a big number in decimal, you simply use a lot of digits. Similarly if you want a big number in **binary** all you need is enough bits. As you can see, this could be one hell of a lot of bits.

Now for adding. Again it works the same way as decimal in all but detail. Decimal uses digits which go up to nine, and if the result of adding two digits together is more than nine you simply 'carry' the overspill digit into the next digit to be added.

For example, 2 7
    + 3 4
    carry 1 because 7+4 overspills
    = 6 1 (the overspill is added to the 2+3)

Similar 'carries' are used in binary, only a bit is going to overspill at the drop of a hat because it only goes up to one:

    0 0 1
    + 1 0 1
    carry 1 because 1+1 overspills
    = 1 1 0

And so on.

As is immediately obvious a computer working in binary is going to spend a lot of time carrying. This is the sort of thing that there is no point worrying about.

To subtract you just do the same backwards, multiplying is just a fancy word for doing an add over and over again, and division is of course easy if you know what the answer is in the first place.

If you want to know why a computer uses binary and not decimal, see **bits.**

SUPPLEMENT 2

Binary/Decimal Conversion

Any value can be represented in either **binary** or decimal.

In decimal the right-most digit counts just as it is. The digit to its left is worth itself times 10, the one to its left is worth itself times 100, the next is worth itself times 1000 and so forth.

In fact, working from the right, this 'multiplying' factor is:

×1 (= 10 to the power of 0)
×10 (= 10 to the power of 1)
×100 (= 10 to the power of 2)
×1000 (= 10 to the power of 3) etc.

Binary values use exactly the same system, but the multiplying factor is a power of 2 rather than 10. The equivalent table for binary is then:

×1 (=2 to the power of 0)
×2 (=2 to the power of 1)
×4 (=2 to the power of 2)
×8 (=2 to the power of 3) etc

Therefore the decimal value of the binary number 00101110 can be worked out by:

(128× **0**)+(64× **0**)+(32× **1**)+(16× **0**)+(8× **1**)+(4× **1**)+(2× **1**)+(1× **0**)=46

Similarly the decimal equivalent of the maximum value of a byte (8 bits all ON, being 11111111) can be calculated by:

(128×1)+(64×1)+(32×1)+(16×1)+(8×1)+(4×1)+(2×1)+(1×1)=255

The **hexadecimal** value of a **semi-byte** can also be worked out using this system, for example:

1001 = (8 × 1) + (4 × 0) + (2 × 0) + (1 × 1) = 9 Decimal = 9 Hexadecimal
1111 = (8 × 1) + (4 × 1) + (2 × 1) + (1 × 1) = 15 Decimal = F Hexadecimal
1100 = (8 × 1) + (4 × 1) + (2 × 0) + (1 × 0) = 12 Decimal = C Hexadecimal